PHILOSOPHY, LITERATURE AND FINE ARTS

ISLAMIC EDUCATION SERIES
Other Titles in the Series

Crisis in Muslim Education
Aims and Objectives of Islamic Education
Social and Natural Sciences: the
Islamic Perspective
Curriculum and Teacher Education
Education and Society in the Muslim World
Muslim Education in the Modern World

General Editor   Syed Ali Ashraf

PHILOSOPHY, LITERATURE AND FINE ARTS

edited by

Seyyed Hossein Nasr

HODDER AND STOUGHTON
KING ABDULAZIZ UNIVERSITY, JEDDAH

British Library Cataloguing in Publication Data

Philosophy, literature and fine arts.—(Islamic
  education series)
  1. Islam—Education
  2. Humanities—Study and teaching—Islamic
  countries
  I. Nasr, Seyyed Hossein   II. Series
  001.3'07'1017671   LB1628

ISBN 0 340 23612 4
First printed 1982
Copyright © 1982 King Abdulaziz University, Jeddah

All rights reserved. No part of this publication may be reproduced or
transmitted in any form or by any means, electronic or mechanical, including
photocopy, recording, or any information storage or retrieval system, without
permission in writing from the publisher.

Typeset by Macmillan India Ltd, Bangalore.
Printed and bound in Great Britain for Hodder and Stoughton Educational, a
division of Hodder and Stoughton Ltd., Mill Road, Dunton Green,
Sevenoaks, Kent by Hazell Watson & Viney Ltd, Aylesbury, Bucks.

Contents

Preface

Introduction

Chapter One	The Teaching of Philosophy — *Seyyed Hossein Nasr*	3
Chapter Two	Islamic Principles and Methods in the Teaching of Literature — *Syed Ali Ashraf*	22
Chapter Three	The Rôle of Fine Arts in Muslim Education — *Ibrahim Titus Burckhardt*	41
Chapter Four	Education in the Traditional Arts and Crafts and the Cultural Heritage of Islam — *Jean-Louis Michon (Ali Abd al-Khaliq)*	51
Chapter Five	On Art and Education — *Kazi A. Kadir*	65
Chapter Six	Translation: Problems and Methods — *Peter Hobson (Ismā'īl 'Abdul-Bāqī)*	73
Chapter Seven	The Teaching of Arabic in the Non-Arabic Speaking Muslim World — *Dr. S. M. Yusuf*	87
Chapter Eight	The Teaching of Languages in Muslim Universities — *Dr. M. M. Ghaly*	109
Appendix	Recommendations of the Committee on Philosophy, Literature and the Arts	118

Preface

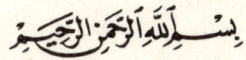

The Pagan Greeks sought unity for all branches of knowledge through their concept of the nine Muses. Their intellectuals, with Socrates, Plato and Aristotle as their leaders, thought that they had discovered this unity in the metaphysical concept of the 'idea'. They therefore considered Metaphysics as the highest form of knowledge. They integrated all branches of knowledge by showing how their basic concepts are rooted in a metaphysical reality. Philosophy was considered to be that branch of knowledge which would help an investigator to realize these roots by leading him into the precincts of metaphysics. Reason was therefore given the highest status and considered to be the means of reaching Truth.

The Greek thinkers had ignored revelation — Islam reasserted revelation as the only means of knowing the Absolute. It laid full emphasis on the spiritual means of contact between God and Man, between Higher Reality and normal day-to-day existence. The Prophet of Islam did not argue or use reason as the primary means of enkindling faith in the hearts of unbelievers. His most intimate companion, Abu Bakr (may Allah be pleased with him), accepted his narration of the Prophet's ascension in Mi'rāj as if he himself had experienced that Reality. Faith thus has a different form of rationale and different *modus operandi*. Muslim philosophers were influenced by Plato and Aristotle. They discussed the comparative importance of revelation and reason. Ghazzālī realized the limitations of reason and fully justified the importance of revelation.

For modern man reason and logic have again become more important than spiritual realisation. He is now suspicious of the validity of revelation. His reason, however, has made him conscious of the fact that all his findings and conclusions are not absolute but tentative. But this realization has not drawn him nearer to revelation and he is still ignoring the Absolute. As a result he and his society have started drifting aimlessly.

It is only when man realizes the importance of his spirit that he will be able to appreciate this significance and value of imagination. If he goes on drifting, if he considers everything as tentative it will not be possible for him to regard some aspects of human personality as more valuable than another. Thus he will not be able to love the 'good' and hate the 'evil'. Even the conflict between good and evil will deteriorate into a kind of conflict in which there will be no hierarchy of values and no settled premise to fall back upon. This is what is happening nowadays in Western literary criticism.

In this book an attempt has been made to indicate in what way Philosophy, Literature and Fine Arts should be treated by educational planners when drawing up the curriculum or training teachers. We are here more concerned with the conceptual aspect than with detailed planning. We hope this will lead to further research in these fields, so that Islamic concepts are formulated in greater detail, and in planning educational courses the place of Philosophy, Literature, Fine Arts and Language is determined more effectively.

Syed Ali Ashraf
General Editor

In the Name of God — Most Merciful,
Most Compassionate

Introduction

Few issues are of greater immediate concern for the Islamic world than education, for it is through the kind of education given or not given to the young that the future of the Islamic community shall be to a large extent determined. It is, therefore, a welcome sign that the First International Conference on Muslim Education had finally taken place and quite rightly at the Blessed City of Makkah where the primary source of all authentic Islamic education, the Holy Qurān, was first revealed. May this type of activity mark a real beginning of the re-appraisal and re-evaluation, according to authentic Islamic criteria, of all the educational institutions, systems and methods existing in the Islamic world today.

Despite the large number of educators who participated in this conference, there is no doubt that many whose views and actions are most effective and influential in educational matters were absent. The publication of the essays and papers delivered in the conference was therefore a matter of necessity. It is hoped that through these publications a much larger community of Muslim scholars, teachers and educators will become aware of the crucial problems involved for the present and future generations of Muslims faced with the unprecedented challenge of a secularized world whose science and know-how most Muslims want to emulate without losing their faith in the process and yet they are at a loss as to how to carry out such a task.

I had the pleasure of participating in the planning of the conference and the honour of chairing the section dealing with the teaching of philosophy and the arts. This section provided some of the most significant and problematic discussions since it dealt with subjects which are more difficult to treat from the point of Islam in a contemporary educational setting than either the purely religious sciences or the natural and mathematical sciences. That is why practically every kind of Islamic university has had its greatest challenge in creating an 'Islamic humanities' or 'Islamic arts and sciences' in order to be able to create a complete Islamic educational system as we see in the Islamic universities of old in which subjects such as philosophy, literature and the arts were taught but in an Islamic context.

Because of the vastness of the subject, it was not possible to deal with every issue involved, but at least the major subjects of philosophy, literature, language and the arts were discussed in our section. The major papers which were presented have been assembled and edited in this collection. But since the text of the paper of Dr. Taftazani on philosophy was not available, an essay on the teaching of philosophy was written by myself expressly for this volume to complete at least the major topics which should be treated in such a work.

It is unfortunate that all the rich discussions which followed the presentation of each paper could not be re-produced here. Nevertheless, these papers written by leading Muslim authorities, some born as Muslims and others Europeans attracted to the wisdom and beauty of Islam and the perfume of the Quranic revelation, represent an important collection which can be of much use to individual teachers as well as educational administrators and even governments planning programmes for Islamic education. It is most of all hoped that educational planners will consider seriously the proposals made in each essay as well as the recommendations of the committee which appears at the end of the book.

The order of the chapters has been decided by Dr. Syed Ali Ashraf, and starts only accidentally with the chapter on philosophy by the editor of the volume. The first five chapters deal with philosophy, literature, the fine arts and the crafts and Islamic culture while the last three deal with the more technical problems of language and translation. All of the chapters are composed by leading authorities who have spent years in the study and practice of the subject with which they are concerned. There are of course other important branches of the humanities such as history which are not represented in this volume. But most such subjects have been dealt with in other volumes in the series.

In conclusion we wish to express our hope that the present volume will play at least some role in awakening the interest and directing the attention of the educators of the Islamic world to the crucial issues involved. May Allah guide those placed in the position of great responsibility of educating Muslim youth to remember always their duties towards the Islamic tradition and the perennial truths for whose sake the Blessed Prophet, that greatest of all Islamic teachers, was chosen to reveal Islam.

wa mā tawfīqī illā bi'Llāh
Seyyed Hossein Nasr

Chapter One

The Teaching of Philosophy

Seyyed Hossein Nasr

Born 1933, Tehran, Iran: Professor of Religion and Islamic Studies, Temple University, Philadelphia. Previously President, Iranian Academy of Philosophy 1975-1979; Chancellor, Aryamehr University 1972-1975; Vice-Chancellor, Tehran University 1970-1971; First Aga Khan Professor of Islamic Studies, American University of Beirut 1964-1965; Professor and Dean of the Faculty of Arts and Letters, Tehran University 1968-1972; Teaching Fellow, Harvard University 1955-1958; publications — twenty one books and over two hundred articles and reviews written in English, French, Persian and Arabic — including: *An Introduction to Islamic Cosmological Doctrines* (1964), *Ideals and Realities of Islam* (1966), *Science and Civilization in Islam* (1968), *The Encounter of Man and Nature* (1968), *Sufi Essays* (1972), *Islam and the Plight of Modern Man* (1976), *Islamic Science, an Illustrated Study* (1976), *An Annotated Bibliography of Islamic Science* (1975/8), *Islamic Life and Thought* (1981).

Before discussing how philosophy should be taught in the Islamic world, it is important to deal with the question whether it should be taught at all because there are many who doubt the usefulness of teaching such a subject or even oppose it completely. If by philosophy we mean modern, Western philosophy, then it can be of course debated with complete justification as to whether this subject should be taught at all to Muslim students as philosophy as such, especially to students who have had no grounding in the Islamic philosophical tradition. But remembering that philosophy is a polysemic term, a word with many meanings, it can be said with certainty that it is not possible to have an educational system without some kind of philosophy, in some sense of the meaning of this term, being taught even if this subject is never mentioned by such a name. One cannot teach physics or chemistry without accepting certain presumptions concerning the nature of reality which are intimately related to seventeenth century European philosophy, nor biology without teaching the student at the same time certain very hypothetical ideas about change, process and so-called evolution, all related to nineteenth century European philosophy. Nor can one study even classical Islamic theology without a knowledge of logic. In fact even in classical Islamic education all students were taught some kind of philosophy, understood here as both a world-view and a method of thinking applicable to various sciences including jurisprudence (*fiqh*). It must, therefore, be accepted that one cannot impart knowledge and have a formal educational system without having some kind of philosophy as both a world-view and a method for the disciplining of the mind. The question, therefore, is not whether one should teach philosophy to Muslim students but what kind or kinds of philosophy should be taught and how this subject should be approached. Lack of attention to this crucial question has caused immeasurable problems in educational institutions throughout the Islamic world and has been one of the main causes for the inability of the contemporary Islamic world to create a properly speaking Islamic educational system which would both be Islamic and would also not shun the questions of a philosophical nature which the modern world poses for Muslims.

If philosophy is to be taught, then one must first decide what is meant by philosophy and what kind of philosophy or philosophies one should teach. For most modernized educated Muslims the term means simply Western philosophy, especially its main current from Descartes, Leibnitz and Malebranch through Locke, Hume, Kant and Hegel to various modern schools of existentialism, positivism and Marxism. Most people have also heard of al-Fārābī or Ibn Sīnā without knowing exactly what they have really said. For many of the traditional Muslims not yet touched by modern education, the term philosophy still implies wisdom, *al-ḥikmah*, which they associate with the prophets as well as the Muslim saints. As for the learned among the traditional segment of Islamic society, those not influenced by the rationalizing movements of the Twelfth and Thirteenth Islamic centuries associated with the name of 'Abd al-Wahhāb and others, philosophy is simply associated with the traditional *falsafah* towards which they have the same traditional attitude as in older days. But few are aware of the fact that in the context of present-day education and the understanding of philosophy, not only is *falsafah* philosophy, but 'philosophy' exists in many other Islamic sciences such as *tafsīr, ḥadīth, kalām, uṣūl al-fiqh, taṣawwuf* and of course the natural and mathematical sciences, all of which are rooted in principle in the Holy Qur'ān which is of course the fountain of *ḥikmah* or wisdom.

In order to define what we mean by philosophy, it is necessary to go beyond this polarization. One cannot consider philosophy as simply modern Western philosophy or accept the appraisal of even the most knowledgeable of Muslim 'reformers', that is, Muḥammad Iqbal when he took certain strands of European philosophy too seriously to the extent that in his *Jāvīd-nāmah* where Rūmī is guiding him in paradise, he comes upon Nietzsche and asserts,

'I said to Rumi, "who is this madman?"
He said, "this is the Wise Man of Germany"'.

Nor can one be completely successful and honest, intellectually speaking, by simply rejecting philosophy as *kufr* and refusing to confront it although most of modern philosophy is in fact *kufr* from the Islamic point of view. This cannot be done because Western philosophical ideas will simply creep through the backdoor in a thousand different ways and students will be much less prepared to confront them or reject alien ideas if they have not been inoculated properly against them through a vigorous study and refutation of their false theses. What must be done is to define philosophy itself from the Islamic point of view and then to re-appraise the current meaning or meanings of philosophy in the light of the Islamic perspective.

It is true that the Islamic intellectual tradition was too rich and diversified to provide just one meaning for the Qurānic term *al-ḥikmah*, it is also true that the several intellectual perspectives cultivated in Islam all conformed to the doctrine of unity (*al-tawḥīd*) and that one can come to an understanding of the meaning of the term, philosophy, as a knowledge about the nature of things leading to and based upon *al-tawḥīd* and therefore being profoundly Islamic even if issuing originally from non-Islamic sources. The view of traditional Islamic philosophers that 'philosophy originates from the lamp of prophecy' derives directly from their basing *al-tawḥīd* as the criterion for the Islamicity of a particular teaching. In any case philosophy could be re-defined according to Islamic standards to preserve its intellectual vigour but at the same time remain attached to the revelation and its central doctrine which is none other than unity. From the very beginning the currently prevailing idea of philosophy as scepticism and doubt, as an individualistic activity of man as a being who has rebelled against God, and as the objectivization of the limitations of a particular human being called a philosopher, should be removed from the minds of students. It should be replaced by the idea of wisdom, universality, certitude and the supra-individual character of not only the Truth as such but also its major traditional formulations and crystallizations so that philosophy becomes identified with an enduring intellectual perspective as it has always been in the East rather than an individualistic interpretation of reality which has been the case of Western philosophy since Descartes.

The teaching of philosophy to Muslim students should begin not only with an Islamic understanding of the meaning of philosophy, but with a thorough study of the whole of the Islamic intellectual tradition. Before the student is exposed to Descartes and Kant or even Plato and Aristotle as seen through the eyes of modern Western philosophy, he or she should receive a thorough grounding in Islamic philosophy and the other disciplines which have a philosophical import. Those devising curricula should have as wide a perspective as possible and go beyond the debilitating attacks of the past century against the Islamic tradition itself which would reduce the great wealth of this tapestry, that is Islamic intellectual life, to simply one of its strands. Whether the planners or the teachers sympathize with the jurisprudents or theologians, the philosophers in the technical sense of *falāsifah* or the Sufis, with critics of logical discourse or its supporters is really besides the point. If there is to be a successful programme of philosophy which would enable the Muslim student to confront modern disciplines, ideologies and points of view without losing his spiritual orientation, then the full force of the Islamic intellectual tradition must be brought into play and the narrowing of perspective avoided.

Even great debates between various Islamic schools of philosophy and thought in general such as those which were carried out between Ibn Sīnā and al-Bīrūnī, Ibn Sīnā, al-Ghazzālī and Ibn Rushd, Naṣīr al-Dīn al-Ṭūsī and Ṣadr al-Dīn al-Qunyawī and many others must be brought out. After all, during the periods of Islamic history when Muslims produced world famous scientists and thinkers such as al-Fārābī, Ibn Sīnā or al-Bīrūnī debates between various perspectives were carried out without these debates harming Islam in any way since they were all within the world-view of the Islamic tradition. The student should be made to know something of this rich intellectual background and not be presented with the Islamic intellectual tradition as a monolithic structure allowing only of one level of interpretation. Such a perspective only deadens the mind and creates a passivity which makes the penetration of foreign ideas into the Islamic world much easier.

The Islamic intellectual tradition should also be taught in its fullness in time. Nothing has been more detrimental to an authentic revival of Islamic thought than the fallacious notion that Islamic thought decayed at the end of the Abbasid period. This interpretation of Islamic history was originally the work of orientalists who could accept Islamic civilization only as a phase in the development of their civilization. The adoption of this view by certain Muslims is, therefore, even more surprising seeing that it does so much injustice to the grandeur of Islamic civilization and, even more importantly, is simply false. It was adopted in certain circles for nationalistic reasons or for political opportunism but surely it cannot be entertained today. How can a civilization which created the Sultan Aḥmad mosque or the Shaykh Luṭfallāh mosque be decadent? Or how on the intellectual plane can one call a Mīr Dāmād or Mullā Ṣadrā a less serious metaphysician than any of their contemporaries anywhere in the world? The presentation of the Islamic intellectual tradition should definitely come up to the present day, brushing aside categorically this false notion of decadence taken from European historical studies of the nineteenth and early twentieth centuries. But this presentation should include discussions of periods when there was a lack of intellectual activity if such were really the case. Those parts of the Islamic world where Muslims were actually 'sleeping over treasures,' to quote a contemporary metaphysician and master of Islamic intellectuality, should be mentioned, but so should also such figures as Shaykh al-Darqāwī, Mullā Hādī Sabziwārī or the philosophers of Farangī Maḥal, all of whom re-kindled various schools of traditional Islamic intellectuality in different parts of the Islamic world during the past two centuries. In fact the so-called Muslim reformers about whom so much has been written should be re-appraised in the light of full knowledge of the Islamic intellectual tradition.

Having gained a thorough knowledge of the Islamic intellectual tradition in its general features, if not in its details, the Muslim student should then be introduced to other schools of philosophy which should include not only Western thought but also Oriental philosophies. No better antidote can be found for the scepticism inherent in much of modern Western philosophy than the traditional doctrines of the Orient which, like Islamic philosophy itself, are philosophy only in the sense of wisdom because oriental doctrines are all based upon the Absolute and the means of attaining the Absolute. They are in a sense various forms of commentary upon the Qur'ānic verse, 'We come from Allah and unto Him is our return' (*innā li' Llāh wa innā ilayhi rāji'ūn*). The Muslim student should be made aware that besides the Islamic world and the all-powerful Western philosophies and ideologies there are several civilizations with their own profound intellectual traditions.

Besides the Orient, ancient Greek philosophy and its antecedents in Egypt and Mesopotamia should be taught not as a part of Western thought but independently as Muslim thinkers have always considered them. It is strange that most Islamic modernists have seen Greek philosophy almost completely through the eyes of its modern Western interpreters. When Iqbal calls Plato 'one of the sheep', he is following more the interpretation of Platonism by Nietzsche than by the Islamic philosophers themselves who saw in Plato and Pythagoras a confirmation of the Islamic doctrine of *al-tawḥīd*. The study of Greek thought according to the Islamic intellectual tradition and independent of its Western interpretation is crucial for the Islamic confrontation with modern Western philosophy itself, whether it be the thought of men like Jaspers and Heidegger who have dealt extensively with the Greeks, or positivists who do not consider anything before Kant, or at best Hume, as being philosophy at all.

The study of non-Islamic schools of thought should also emphasize Christian and Jewish philosophy in the European Middle Ages and their later continuation. Not only should such medieval figures as St. Bonaventure, St. Thomas, Duns Scotus, Maimonides and Ibn Gabirol who were also very close to Islamic thought be well known to Muslim students, but much more attention should be paid in philosophy courses in the Islamic world to the later continuation of these schools. Instead of just relegating Christian and Jewish philosophy to the medieval period and following immediately with secularized modern philosophy as is the case today, more emphasis should be placed upon the continuation of these schools not only through Suarez and Spinoza but into the Twentieth century with such figures as E. Gilson and J. Maritain, and H. A. Wolfson and D. Hartman. The purpose of this exercise would be to demonstrate to the Muslim student who might be rapidly carried off his feet as a result of his encounter with modern Western philosophy, how despite the weakening of religion in the West, religious or 'prophetic' philosophy, in many ways similar to the Islamic and based on God and revelation, have continued to this day. Of course in such an enterprise thoroughly anti-traditional but outwardly 'Christian' philosophies such as Teilhardism should also be exposed for what they are.

Finally as far as the development of Western philosophy is concerned, emphasis should be placed upon what has been called the 'anti-history of anti-philosophy', namely, those more traditional schools of philosophy which remained on the margin of European thought and which are not usually discussed in standard texts of the history of Western philosophy employed in Western universities or those of the Islamic world. The research of the past few decades have revealed that certain forms of non-rationalistic philosophy such as Hermeticism survived much more in the Renaissance and the Seventeenth century than had been thought before and that such schools as the Kabbalah, the Rosicrucian movement, Hermeticism and the like were even influential in the rise of experimental science to a degree hitherto unsuspected. Giordano Bruno, Paracelsus, Basil Valentine, Robert Fludd and many similar figures are seen to be of much greater significance even from the point of view of science than the rationalistic interpretations of earlier days had made everyone to believe.

It is important to make Muslim students aware of these elements since such philosophies are both akin in structure and related through historical sources to various schools of Islamic thought.

As for later centuries, more should be said about such figures as Jacob Böhme, Goethe as a philosopher, Schelling, von Baader, St. Martin and many other figures who are also attracting much attention in the contemporary West itself in quest of the re-discovery of the *sophia* which much of its own so-called philosophy denies or abhors.

Since it is primarily modern Western thought which is the source of doubt and scepticism for the educated Muslim, it is essential to acquaint the Muslim student fully with the criticisms made against this thought in the West itself. It has always been said that the cure for a snake bite is the poison of the snake itself. In the same way the best antidote against the errors which constitute the essence — and not necessarily all of the accidents — of what is characteristically modern in contrast to contemporary thought, can be found in the criticisms made in the West itself. To be sure, certain profound criticisms have come from the East, but for the most part Orientals have been either too enfeebled as a result of the process of Westernization itself to stand totally on their own ground, or unable to reach the heart of the problems involved as a result of the lack of knowledge of the inner workings of Western thought. The few profound criticisms from the East such as those of the incomparable Indian metaphysician and scholar A. K. Coomaraswamy have been an exception rather than the rule.

From the West, however, has come a total and complete criticism of the very structure of modern thought. These criticisms include majesterial expositions based on traditional authority and grounded on thorough knowledge of traditional metaphysics and philosophy such as the *Oriental Metaphysics* of R. Guénon and *Logic and Transcendence* of F. Schuon as well as a description of the 'malaise' inherent in modern philosophy and thought by a large number of notable thinkers in quest of the re-discovery of the Truth, a task from which many critics believe the mainstream of European philosophy to have departed since the Renaissance. Such men include philosophers as well as scientists and men of letters, such figures of E. Zolla in Italy, H. Corbin, G. Durand and A. Faivre in France, H. Smith and Th. Roszak in America and many others. They also include those such as E. Gilson who have written histories of Western philosophy from the point of view of Thomist ontology and epistemology and who have seen in the history of Western thought a gradual fall of the role of philosophy as the study of Being, or of the One who alone *is* in the absolute sense. The Muslim student should be presented with these criticisms while studying the history of Western thought so that he is able to gain certain intellectual concepts necessary to protect himself from the withering effect of agnosticism and doubt associated with so much of modern philosophy.

In teaching philosophy, then, Islamic philosophy should be made central and other schools of philosophy taught in relation to it. Also the method of reducing philosophy to the history of philosophy is itself something completely modern and non-Islamic. Nor in fact does it conform to the perspective of any of the other major traditional civilizations. In such civilizations philosophy is not identified with an individual who gives his name to a particular philosophical mode of thought which is then called for example Cartesianism, Hegelianism, etc. but which is almost immediately criticized and rejected by a subsequent philosopher. Rather, philosophy is identified with an intellectual perspective which lasts over the centuries and which far from being a barrier to creativity remains a viable means of access to the Truth within the tradition in question. Men who give their names to traditional schools of thought are seen more as 'intellectual functions' than mere individuals. Such a situation was also found in the West when it was Christian; for centuries people followed the Augustinian, Thomistic or Palamite schools of theology and philosophy and these schools were seen, and still continue to be seen to the extent that Christian philosophy is alive, as intellectual perspectives transcending the individualistic order. In traditional India and China the situation has of course always been of this kind; namely, wisdom or philosophy has been identified with the name of a great sage, whether he be a historical or a mythical figure, who has opened up an intellectual perspective of a supra-individualistic order surviving over the centuries far beyond the life span of the founder or his disciples.

Islamic philosophy should also be taught in a morphological manner as schools rather than as a continuous history of individual philosophers and their philosophies, as has been the case in many books written even by Muslims themselves but emulating completely Western models. Islamic intellectual life should be divided into its traditional schools of *uṣūl, kalām, mashshā'ī* (Peripatetic) philosophy, *ishrāq* (the School of Illumination), *ma'rifah* or *'irfān* (theoretical and doctrinal Sufism) and finally the later school of *al-ḥikmat al-muta'āliyah* (the Transcendent Theosophy) associated with the name of Ṣadr al-Dīn Shīrāzī. Then each of these schools should be subdivided according to their traditional divisions, such as Sunnī and Shī'ite *uṣūl*, Mu'tazilite, Ash'arite, Ithnā 'asharī and Ismā'īlī *kalām*, Eastern and Western schools of *mashshā'ī* philosophy, etc.

Also each school should be taught according to its own traditional methods, that is, beginning with principles which are always related to the Holy Qur'ān and *Ḥadīth* and followed by the application and development of these principles. Only after the intellectual structure is made known should a historical account be given of each school, a historical account which should come up to the present day, if that school has survived until now as is in fact the case for nearly all Islamic intellectual disciplines provided the whole of the Islamic world is considered and not only its central lands. For example, once the Mu'tazilite school is presented in its doctrinal and philosophical aspects, its historical unfolding would be taught not as ending with Qāḍī 'Abd al-Jabbār in the 5th/11th century but as including the whole later development of this school among the Zaydīs of the Yemen up to modern times and finally its revival among certain of the theologians of al-Azhar during this century.

In the same manner the development of *mashshā'ī* philosophy should not stop with Ibn Rushd as is usually the case, following Western sources for which Islamic philosophy ends with him, but include the later Turkish criticisms of his *Tahāfut al-tahāfut* during the Ottoman period, the revival of *mashshā'ī* philosophy in the East by Naṣīr al-Dīn al-Ṭūsī and Quṭb al-Dīn al-Shīrāzī and the continuation of the school of Ibn Sīnā up to our own times when major philosophical commentaries and analyses of his work have continued to appear in Persia, Pakistan and India. The same could be said of the other schools.

Of course this task is not an easy one because of the state of present day knowledge of Islamic intellectual life in its totality. The detailed development of every one of these schools remains unknown if the whole of the Islamic world is considered. There may be Malay scholars who know how *kalām* developed in their part of the Islamic world as there may still be scholars in Mali who can provide knowledge for the development of the metaphysics of the school of Ibn 'Arabī in that region. But there is no-one nor any one centre of research where all of this knowledge has been brought together. Yet, once it is realized how important it is to provide a total and complete map of Islamic intellectual life in both space and time for current Muslim students, it is not difficult to provide the means to carry out the task of studying these schools, beginning with the traditional method of presenting, first, their principles, and then branches and details, and only later their development in history — a method which will help to avoid this relativization of the Truth and the reduction of all permanence to 'becoming', which is implied within the very methods by which philosophy has been studied and taught in the West. Of course, even in this question, the anti-historicism of certain current Western thinkers can be a help in preventing Muslims from falling into the trap of historicism without being in any way against historical facts. After all, al-Bīrūnī and Ibn Khaldūn were very keen historians without reducing all truths to their history and all permanence to 'becoming'.

The traditional conflict between various schools of Islamic thought should also be taught as conflicts between so many different perspectives converging upon the Truth, conflicts which are of a very different nature from those found between contending philosophical schools in the modern world because in the first case there are always the transcendent principles of the Islamic tradition which ultimately unify, whereas in the second case such unifying principles are missing. It is true that the Ash'arites opposed the Mu'tazilites, that the *mutakallimūn* in general were against the *mashshā'ī* philosophers, that Suhrawardī, the founder of the school of *ishrāq*, criticized Peripatetic logic and metaphysics, that Ibn Taymiyyah wrote against formal logic and Sufism, etc. But had these conflicts been like those of modern thought, the Islamic tradition would not have survived. There was, however, always the unifying principle of *al-tawḥīd*, and a sense of hierarchy within the Islamic tradition itself which allowed intellectual figures to appear from time to time who were at once *mutakallim*, philosopher and metaphysician of the gnostic school (*al-ma'rifah*) and who realized the inner unity of these perspectives within their own being. The fact that there were many and not just one school of thought should not therefore be taught to students as a sign of either chaos or weakness but as the result of the richness of the Islamic tradition, which was able to cater to the needs of different intellectual types and therefore to keep within its fold so many human beings of different backgrounds and intellectual ability. The diversity should be taught as so many applications of the teachings of Islam, some more partial and some more complete, yet all formulated so as to prevent men with different mental abilities and attitudes from seeking knowledge and answers to questions outside the structure of the Islamic tradition itself, as was to happen in the Christian West during the Renaissance. This profusion and diversity of schools which were different but all of which drew from the fountain of the Quranic revelation and *al-tawḥīd* was the means whereby Islam succeeded in preserving the sacred character of knowledge while creating a vast civilization where the development of various modes of knowledge and different sciences was a necessity.

The study of Islamic philosophy in this manner should be complemented by the study of the different questions and subjects of philosophy with which the contemporary student is usually faced. For students of different disciplines such as law, medicine, and the like, those questions such as the nature of the world, causality and the relation between creation and God, could be fitted into the general programme of the study of philosophy within the matrix of the different schools cited above. But for those who will study philosophy itself, or the religious sciences on the one hand and certain of the sciences such as physics on the other, it would be very helpful and perhaps necessary to deal with these subjects separately and morphologically. Even in the Western philosophical syllabus students still study logic, aesthetics, ethics, social and political philosophy, and in many places metaphysics, cosmology and philosophical psychology.

From a pedagogical point of view it is important to deal separately with these disciplines for particular groups of students concerned with the subjects mentioned above, as well as with general courses on Islamic intellectual life along lines described already. It is also obviously essential to teach in a more fully developed and thorough manner Islamic political philosophy to students of political science, philosophy of art and aesthetics to students of art and architecture, the Islamic philosophy of science to students studying all the various natural and mathematical sciences, and so on. In such cases, each discipline should be taught from the Islamic point of view and then the views of Western or non-Islamic Eastern schools should also be presented and, when in contradiction to the Islamic teachings, criticized and explained. In nearly every branch of philosophy the Islamic tradition is rich beyond belief, if only its sources are made known. This is especially true of metaphysics. Here Islamic metaphysics should be presented as the science of Ultimate Reality which is the One (*al-Aḥad*) or Allāh Who has revealed Himself in the Holy Quran. There has been no Islamic school whose teachings are not based on the doctrine of the One who is both Absolute and Infinite. In the study of this Sublime Principle the Muslim sages developed several languages of discourse, some based on the consideration of the One as Pure Being with an ensuing ontology conforming to that view, but always seeing Pure Being not as the first link in the 'great chain of being' but as the Source which transcends all existents. Others saw the One as Light (*al-nūr*) according to the Quranic verse, 'Allah is the Light of the Heavens and the earth', and yet others as the Truth (*al-Ḥaqq*) which transcends even Pure Being, as the supra-ontological Principle whose first determination or act is in fact Being, for Allah said, 'be (*kūn*)' and there was. It is the Western scholars of Islamic philosophy who have called Ibn Sīnā 'the first philosopher of being'; without any exaggeration or chauvinism one could say that in a sense the development of ontology in the West is a commentary on or footnote to Ibn Sīnā, but one which moves towards an ever more limited understanding until finally it results in either the neglect of ontology or a parody of it. Even the present day *Existenz Philosophie*, identified with men like Heidegger, seems like a rudimentary discussion about love by someone who has never experienced it when compared to the philosophy of Being of a figure like Ṣadr al-Dīn Shīrāzī who writes about Being only after having drowned in the Ocean of Pure Being and after purification having been endowed with a sanctified intellect which alone can speak of this Ocean.

In other philosophical subjects such as logic and epistemology also, the Islamic tradition presents an immense richness which should be first resuscitated and then taught to students. Only then should the various modern schools of logic and discussions of the question of knowing be presented. These are of course certain problems of contemporary concern which have no antecedent in Islamic thought and it would be a falsification of the truth and in fact the betrayal of the Islamic tradition to read these problems and their solutions back into the Islamic sources and find allusions to cybernetics, Riemanian space or modern information theory in these sources when in actuality none exists. But even in these cases a mind disciplined in the Islamic sciences would be able to approach such subjects from the point of view of Islamic thought rather than as a *tabula rasa*. There are of course other concerns of a particularly modern nature such as semantics and the question of causality in which the Islamic tradition is remarkably rich. In such instances the Islamic teachings could be presented first and only then the current — and of course ever-changing — modern theories and views taught to those students who have to be concerned with such matters.

The modern world does not possess a cosmology in the real sense of the term but there are many theories about the Universe based on the generalization of contemporary physics. In Islamic civilization, however, several forms of cosmology were developed, all related to the basic teachings of the Holy Qurān concerning the creation of the world by God, the higher planes of being associated with *malakūt* in the Holy Quran, etc. These cosmologies, which are of an eminently symbolic character and which cannot be negated by any form of modern physics and astronomy, should be first taught to students along with their full metaphysical and religious significance which would also explain such events as the nocturnal ascension (*al-miʿrāj*) of the Blessed Prophet. Only after the student is made to have a 'feeling' and an intellectual appreciation of the Islamic Universe should he be exposed to various modern forms of so-called cosmology, all of which should be presented for exactly what they are, namely theories based upon certain questionable and usually empirically unprovable assumptions.

A student should also be taught the various schools of the Islamic 'philosophy of nature' which are closely related to cosmology. These schools have views concerning time, space, matter, change, cause and effect and many other subjects which form the basis of the natural sciences and which in fact have attracted the attention of several important contemporary Western scientists and philosophers of science. As modern physics is in quest of a new 'philosophy of nature', the Islamic teachings on this subject are of the utmost importance for Muslim students of the sciences and perhaps even in the development of a new type of physics or science of nature sought by many perceptive minds today. The same could be said of Islamic works on the philosophy of mathematics, which have hardly been studied in modern times.

Likewise in philosophical psychology, Islamic sources are replete with teachings which are of great value in the confrontation of questions posed in psychology today. In this field, material can be drawn all the way from Quranic commentaries and the *Ḥadīth* to Sufi ethical and psychological tracts, not to speak of the philosophical psychology of the philosophers themselves such as Ibn Sīnā and works of Islamic medicine.

In the philosophy of art or aesthetics, the teaching of the Islamic perspective is important not only from the educational point of view but also because of the effect that the training of Muslim students of art and architecture in Western ways has upon the destruction of the Islamic character of cities and the way of life of the people within the Islamic world. Islamic art is not accidentally Islamic. Rather, it is a direct crystallization of the spirit and form of the Islamic revelation complementing the *Sharī'ah*. One supplies the Islamic mode of action and the other the Islamic environment in which the spirit of Islam breathes and which provides the necessary background for an Islamic way of life. If Islamic art were only accidentally related to Islam, one could not observe and feel the unmistakable fragrance of the Islamic revelation in mosques or handicrafts of lands as far apart as Bengal and the Senegal.

Until recently oral traditions and the homogeneity of the Islamic environment did not necessitate an explicit formulation of the philosophy of Islamic art. But now along with the teaching of the techniques of Islamic art, it is essential to formulate and teach the principles of the philosophy or wisdom (*al-ḥikmah*) which underlies Islamic art, remembering that Islamic art is the fruit of the marriage between technique (*al-fann*) and wisdom (*al-ḥikmah*). This is especially necessary today since modern theories of art and aesthetics, and works based upon them, have engulfed much of the Islamic world and corrode the soul and weaken the faith of Muslims in a direct manner that is often more insidious and pervasive than anti-religious ideologies. These are more easily seen to be what they are whereas many Muslims are unaware of the religious danger of anti-traditional art forms and therefore display a remarkable passivity towards their destructive nature.

In the practical aspects of philosophy such as ethics and political and social philosophies, once again Islamic sources possess an immense richness. Here, as before, the various schools should be presented as so many elaboratives and themes upon the teachings of the Holy Quran and the *Ḥadīth*. For example, Islamic ethics itself is of course based upon these twin sources of Islamic revelation. But there are elaborations of ethics, as a science or a branch of philosophy, in works as different as *al-Risālat al-qushayriyyah* of Imām Qushayrī, sections of *al-Mughnī* of Qāḍī 'Abd al-Jabbār dealing with ethics, many works of Islamic literature such as the *Kalīlah wa dimnah* and the *Gulistān* of Sa 'dī, the *Iḥyā' 'ulūm al-dīn* of al-Ghazzālī, and the *Akhlāq-i nāṣirī* of Naṣīr al-Dīn al-Ṭūsī, all aiming to inculcate the virtues taught in Islam within the soul of man but each providing a different type of ethical theory and method. In such a field as ethics it is even easier than the fields mentioned above to teach first the different schools of Islamic ethics and only then the current ethical theories of Western philosophers or Confucian and Buddhist ethics for that matter, which, too, should be studied.

As for political and social philosophies, there too the Islamic sources are very diverse embracing not only books of philosophy but those dealing with history and literature as well as of course works of jurisprudence (*fiqh*) and the different branches of the law. In these fields a certain amount of work has been already done in presenting students with the views of various Islamic schools before embarking upon the teaching of Western theories. Unfortunately, however, in many cases instead of presenting the different Islamic schools objectively in all their diversity and richness, often local political conditions have been chosen as criteria of what schools should be taught. Even among Western ideologies only those are studied which are closer to the political stance of the particular Muslim state in question whereas all the different Western schools of political and social philosophy which have been, or are, of any consequence should be studied and criticized from the stance of the Islamic tradition so that the student feels secure within his own tradition no matter which type of modern philosophy he confronts. For example, if the laissez-faire type of social and political philosophy is studied and rejected from the Islamic point of view but the Marxist is left untouched and passed over in silence, the Muslim student may be completely unequipped intellectually when confronted with the latter and not be able to defend his position before its arguments or the arguments of those pseudo-syntheses which would try to combine the Islamic and the Marxist views into a supposed unity, as if ice and fire could be made to exist harmoniously side by side.

The implementation of the programme outlined above requires of course educational planning, training of qualified individuals as both teachers and research scholars, collecting of manuscripts and the composition of books and monographs at various levels. As far as educational planning is concerned, it must be said at the outset that obviously Islamic philosophy should be taught to students who have already studied the principles of Islam, the Holy Qurān, *Hadīth*, the sacred history of Islam and at least some aspects of *fiqh* and *usūl al-fiqh* even if in rudimentary fashion. In this way the mind of the student would be impregnated with Islamic values and norms and he could confront alien elements accordingly. But if philosophy is taught in the manner outlined above, this function will also be performed by the various schools of Islamic philosophy themselves. Ibn Sīnā was already thoroughly educated in the purely Islamic disciplines before confronting Aristotelian metaphysics; therefore his works can help the student and strengthen the student's own Islamic intellectual formation before he faces the works of a Hegel or Heidegger with whom classical Islamic philosophy was not obviously familiar. But if the Islamic intellectual tradition is put aside and the student is presented with only the Holy Qurān and *Hadīth* from which he is expected to deduce his own 'philosophy of Islam,' then such a plan can never succeed. At best the student will shy away from problems posed by modern thought in order to protect his faith and at worst he will be overcome by what, for an untrained person, is an overwhelming challenge. As a result he will either lose his faith or end up with some kind of a pseudo-synthesis of Islam and different modern ideologies which is often more insidious and dangerous than the loss of faith.

As far as educational programming for the teaching of Islamic philosophy is concerned, it must begin on the secondary and even elementary level and not be limited solely to the university. From the earliest grades reference in text books for Muslim children should be primarily to Muslim men of learning. Biographies of great sages and thinkers such as al-Ghazzālī, 'Abd al-Qādir al-Jīlānī, al-Fārābī, Ibn Sīnā, al-Bīrūnī, and Ibn Khaldūn, should impregnate the history and cultural programmes of the earlier years of education following directly upon the study of the life of Blessed Prophet, the companions, imams of the *madhāhib* and for Shi'ism, the Shi'ite Imams, etc. Moreover, the vast popular literature concerning many Islamic intellectual figures should be included.

In later years of secondary education names of major books of Islamic thought and a few of the basic ideas and debates such as those mentioned above should be added. Finally for the last two years programmes of elements of philosophy based on the study of logic, some principles of metaphysics and ethics, a brief intellectual history of the various schools, etc. should be devised thoroughly on Islamic lines as, for example, the French and German educational systems have done for the *lycée* and the *gymnasium* but on purely European lines. Only then should something be said in the programme for Muslim students about Western and possibly even Oriental philosophies. But the treatment of Western thought, although very elementary at this stage, should still be critical and not apologetic or defensive.

As for university education, there must be several types of programmes: one for those majoring in philosophy, another for those whose field is close to philosophy such as theology and other religious disciplines including both Islamic Law and comparative religion, another for those majoring in the theoretical sciences such as physics and mathematics, another for descriptive sciences such as biology, ecology and geology, another for students of the social sciences, another for the arts, and so on. The details of such programmes need careful study and cannot be provided here, but the general aim of Islamizing an education system by making its intellectual perspective and world-view totally Islamic can be pointed out and emphasized even before studying the details of implementation.

The training of personnel for such a programme poses a major problem at the present moment but not one which is insurmountable. At the present time only a handful of the traditional masters of Islamic philosophy who connect the present generation to the days of Suhrawardī and Ibn Sīnā continue to survive. The oral traditions which they still possess and which complement the written texts are a most precious treasure of Islamic intellectual life. Before such people disappear altogether from the surface of the earth, it is essential to choose a number of gifted students and provide the means for both the teachers and the students to make this vital training and transmission possible. But scholars with more contemporary training though experts in Islamic intellectual disciplines are very limited in number. There are not enough people to staff even the major universities of the Islamic world. Therefore, every effort should be made to create institutions, academic societies, etc., which will bring such experts into contact with qualified students. To train such students, it is necessary to create both the atmosphere and a minimum number of qualified teachers who would in fact attract good students through their own presence. Personal efforts in this direction have produced satisfactory results in the past. With all the funds now available in the Islamic world, it should not be difficult to finance a few such centres whose students could later become the professors of universities and train men and women who would in turn teach at the secondary and even elementary levels.

An urgent task, of much importance for a full understanding of the various dimensions and the immense richness of Islamic thought, is the collection and preservation of manuscripts concerning Islamic philosophy, metaphysics and related subjects. Most of these manuscripts are in Arabic but a large number are in Persian and a few in other Islamic languages such as Turkish, Urdu and Malay. Despite the laudable efforts of various public and semi-public libraries as well as of the Arab League centre for Arabic manuscripts in Cairo, and despite the collection on Islamic medicine and related sciences which is being assembled by the Hamdard Institute in Delhi, a great deal needs to be accomplished in bringing together manuscripts in private collections which are in danger of being lost or destroyed. This is especially a problem in the Indo-Pakistani sub-continent which is extremely rich in Islamic manuscripts but is at the same time endowed with a humid and warm climate which causes manuscripts to decay and disintegrate very rapidly if they are not well stored and cared for. While this work is being undertaken, copies should be made of manuscripts dealing with Islamic philosophy and related subjects and collected in a few centres created for the advanced study of Islamic philosophy.

As far as books and monographs are concerned, so much needs to be done that it needs a separate study to deal even with the outline of the work involved. Here it suffices to point out some of the major projects which need to be pursued. First of all the work of a group of Muslim and also Western scholars who have performed the thankless task of editing the actual texts of Islamic thought must be continued in force so that within a few years there will be available the complete works or *Opera Omnia* of at least the major Islamic intellectual figures such as al-Ghazzālī, Ibn Sīnā and Ibn Khaldūn. Islamic civilization lags far behind others including Japan and India in publishing its literary treasures and still today there is not a single major Islamic intellectual figure all of whose writings can be found in a critical edition.

At the same time dictionaries must be compiled of philosophical and scientific terminology in Islamic languages with greater co-operation between scholars of these languages than has been the case until now. Some activity has taken place in this field by the Arab Academy and several Iranian organizations but much remains to be accomplished before philosophy, including Western thought, can be taught to Muslim students in their own languages and in a way which remains faithful to the genius of those languages and their traditional roots. The secularization of thought is always closely related to the secularization of language.

The question of language is so essential that it is necessary in some cases to re-write classical works in a contemporary medium, especially for students, while preserving the classical technical vocabulary to the extent possible. Not only is there an urgent need to translate the major masterpieces of Islamic metaphysics and philosophy such as the *Kitāb al-hurūf* of al-Fārābī, *al-Najāt* of Ibn Sīnā, *Tahāfut al-falāsifah* of al-Ghazzālī, *Hikmat al-ishrāq* of Suhrawardī, *Fuṣūṣ al-hikam* of Ibn ʿArabī, *al-Insān al-kāmil* of ʿAbd al-Karīm al-Jīlī and *al-Shawāhid al-rubūbiyyah* of Ṣadr al-Dīn Shīrāzī from Arabic into various Islamic languages (part of this task has already been accomplished with varying degrees of success), but such works should be rewritten in contemporary Arabic in such a way as to preserve the original technical vocabulary and at the same time to be rendered more open and available to the contemporary Arab student. Many classical recensions in fact performed the same task for people of other centuries.

The teaching of philosophy also requires works to be composed on the basis of these traditional sources but dealing with more specific subjects such as metaphysics, ethics, aesthetics, etc. Such treatises written from the Islamic point of view are rare indeed although a few fine examples can be found in Arabic, Persian and even Urdu. Treatises of this kind must be written at different levels so as to reach the whole spectrum of students. In the more advance works of this kind comparisons can also be made with non-Islamic thought although separate works on 'comparative philosophy' remain essential.

Muslims have been somewhat more successful in writing histories of philosophy, if one judges by numbers. Such works, emulating mostly Western models, range from the large two-volume history edited by M. M. Sharif and sponsored by the Pakistani government to individual efforts of much more modest dimensions. Still, the Islamic world has not been able to produce such definitive and thorough works on the history of Islamic thought as those produced by Indian, Chinese and Japanese scholars on their own traditions. What are needed in the case of Islamic thought are many more monograph studies which would make known so many areas which are still *terra incognita*. A few years ago one could hardly imagine that the anthology prepared by H. Corbin and S. J. Āshtiyānī of Islamic philosophy just in Persia and only since the Safavid period would become some seven heavy volumes with many basic selections left out because of the unmanageable size of each volume.

Finally, the teaching of Islamic philosophy requires the preparation of encyclopedias and philosophical dictionaries such as those available for not only Western but also the Indian and Japanese traditions. At the present moment knowledge about many facets of Islamic thought is not easily accessible and is certainly beyond the means of students, even if they be advanced. Considering that Muslims were accustomed to composing encyclopedias dealing with various subjects such as the Muʿtazilite encyclopedia *al-Mughnī* of Qāḍī ʿAbd al-Jabbār, the *Shifāʾ*, of Ibn Sīnā or the *Biḥār al-anwar* of Majlisī, it is even more difficult to understand why this tradition has not been pursued in our own day. In the field of intellectual life, certainly, it is badly needed.

Of course the Islamic world cannot wait until all these tasks are accomplished before Islamic philosophy is taught seriously in the educational systems of the Muslim world. Time is in fact a most important factor because the withering influence of secularizing ideologies and false philosophies continues to erode the foundations of the Islamic tradition before our eyes. Every effort should therefore be used to do what one can here and now. It must be remembered that the greatest obligation of the Muslim is towards the Truth (*al-Ḥaqq*) which is another name of Allah. From this Truth or *al-ḥaqīqah* has issued not only a Sacred Law which guarantees human felicity on the plane of action but also a wisdom which is the guarantee of knowing correctly and keeping upon the straight path of knowledge. The loss of this wisdom cannot but affect the understanding and mode of attachment of men to the Sacred Law. The teaching of Islamic philosophy in the sense defined above is the means of protecting that Truth and providing ways for repelling the attacks which are made against it from all sides. Its teaching in the correct manner is, therefore, in a sense a religious duty, for any step taken in the understanding of *al-ḥaqīqah* as well as in providing means to protect it from profanation, distortion and obliteration lies at the heart of the concerns of Islam as the message and the embodiment of the Truth for whose sake alone human beings were created and placed on earth as the vice-gerents of Allah.

Chapter Two

Islamic Principles and Methods in the Teaching of Literature

Syed Ali Ashraf

Born Bengal 1925; educated at Dacca (M.A. in English) and Cambridge University (B.A. Hons., M.A. and Ph.D.). Director-General, World Centre for Islamic Education, Makkah, and Professor of English, King Abdulaziz University, Jedda, Saudi Arabia. Previously he was Professor and Head of the Department of English, King Abdulaziz University, Makkah (1974–77); Visiting Fellow, Clare Hall, Cambridge (1973–74); Reader and Head, (1956–65) Professor and Head, Karachi University English Department (1965–72); Reader and Head, English Department, Rajshahi University (1954–56). He was also a Visiting Professor at Harvard University, Summer 1971, and at New Brunswick University, Canada, Summer 1974. His publications include: (in English): *T.S. Eliot Through Pakistani Eyes*; *New Harmony* (an anthology of Pakistani poetry in English); *Muslim Tradition in Bengali Literature*, *Homage to Nazrul Islam*; *Venture* (a quarterly, then a bi-annual journal of English language and literature, 1958–72); *Bengali Literary Review* (1971–73); (in Bengali); *Kavya Parichay* (a comparative study of Western and Eastern Poetics); *Kavya-Sankalan* (an edition of Golam Mostata's poems with an introduction); two books of Bengali poems *Chaitra Jakhan* and *Visangati*.

I

Definition

Literature is a form of human activity. No human activity is neutral in character. It is either good or bad or a mixture of the two. Even that which is good is only predominantly good and that which is bad is only predominantly bad. No human activity is entirely good or entirely bad because only God is absolutely good and Satan is completely bad. The question arises, is literature good? If it is not, then we should not teach it. If it is, then we must find out in what way it is good. This means that we shall have to define in concrete terms what literature means and what its function is.

Literature is that form of writing which man creates with the help of language in order to enjoy his exploration of the experience of life. Its basic characteristic is its fictional quality. The writer creates an image of life in order to enshrine in it his understanding of the meaning of life derived from his experience. Science is factual because it investigates facts and concludes from data thus collected. A writer responds to the facts of life and presents to readers the resultant intuitive realization of Truth. This realization is presented always through some attractive image of life which symbolises experiential reality. Thus Truth is garbed in the image of beauty and presented to us in order to lead us unto the author's realisation of the meaning of existence. This beautiful image is fictional in character and not factual. Poetry, the novel and drama are the most attractive forms so far evolved as moulds for those images.

II

Literature as a Form of Knowledge

Literature is thus a form of knowledge. This knowledge is partial but sincere and genuine. It is partial because it is only an individual's experience of reality. As that individual is a human being, his experience can never be complete. Only Allah possesses complete knowledge. But as experience is continually expanding, this knowledge is also continually advancing and expanding. This expansion of knowledge means a continual re-creation of the self because knowledge of anything other than the self is a means of making anything other than self a part of one's self. It is through this self-awareness that man becomes conscious of his relationship with God, with nature and with the world at large. It is within this self that the essence of Man lies hidden, the essence about which Allah has said, 'I have breathed within him from my own Spirit.'[1] It is this awareness that was granted to Adam (peace be upon him) by Allah when He taught him the 'the Names' of everything.[2] The 'names of things' ultimately means the 'essence of things' and the essence of everything is nothing but the manifestation of the different powers of Allah Himself. Thus all the Names of Allah were implanted within him and Adam (peace be upon him) became *khalīfatullāh* (vice-gerent of God) by thus being able to represent all the attributes of Allah expressed through His Names. The highest form of self-awareness therefore is the awareness of these attributes and through them all the essences related to the great Reality which is manifested by Allah Himself. It is only from this point of view that everything in the Universe is regarded as Signs of God — '*āyatallāh*'.

But the awareness of this reality is not easily accessible to every individual because of the nature granted to man by Allah. On the one hand Allah has created man in the best possible image (*aḥsan al-taqwīm*)[3] and given him Divine Spirit (*wa nafakhtu fihi min rūḥī*).[4] On the other hand He has place man in the world of matter and given him a passionate soul attached to his body (*al-nafs al-ammārah*)[5] which tempts him towards the lowest of the low (*asfal al-sāfilīn*).[6] The great evil power, Satan, has not been stopped by Allah from trying to tempt man from the path of righteousness.[7] Thus man is constantly in conflict within himself and with forces surrounding him. Therefore, the norm of righteousness revealed to man by Allah through His chosen Prophets (peace be upon them) can be responded to by the Divine Spirit which is within man. At the same time the norm of selfishness, which evil powers within himself and outside him tempt him to accept for his temporary gain in this world, creates a conflict in his mind. It is this conflicting situation that attracts the writer's attention. He realises how complex this conflict is. Imagination (*khayāl*) is that faculty within man which helps him to see the inter-relationship among various experiences, and perceptions. It also synthesises his perceptions and thus enables him to see the unity that exists behind the apparently divided and fragmented universe. Thus man's different senses bring different kinds of perceptions when he sees or perceives, for example, a table. But he is able to think of the table as a unit only because his imagination has helped him to unify his perceptions of colours, shape, form and touch and give to his mind the concept of a unified object. This concept of unity is ultimately derived from the concept of Divine Unity (*al-tawḥīd*) which the Divine power within man enables him to realise. Poetic imagination is the creative ability which helps man to break the rigid time and space association that memory imposes upon the series of experiences that man acquires and to recreate a new world out of the world of these experiences in order to give to readers a beautiful image through which his vision of reality is expressed.

In other words, imagination is that faculty within man's self which establishes the relationship between the Spirit and the self and hence between spiritual reality and material existence. Therefore it enables man to re-integrate sense perceptions, intellectual formulations and spiritual realisations into new wholes and thus present his own image in different forms and colours. Imagination must be regarded, therefore, as a factor which unifies. But imagination at one level works as a force that unites and synthesises impressions. At the creative level, it cannot be productive of anything of value if it does not listen to the meaning of experience that the spiritual self reveals to it. This revelation is marred by extraneous elements which become cluttered in a man's self because of his continuous intercourse with daily events. That is why it is necessary for a writer to purify his self, to be detached and not attached to any impression. But detachment without faith in a Higher Reality, without any conviction in God who alone reveals correct intimations, builds up images without revealing them with certainty. This same idea has been expressed by Ananda K. Coomaraswamy in almost similar words as follows:

> 'In the production of anything made by art, two faculties, respectively imaginative and operative, free and servile, are simultaneously involved; the former consisting of the conception of some ideal inimitable form, the latter in the imitation (*mimesis*) of this invisible model (*paradeigma*) in some material, which is then informed. The distinctive character of all the arts is, accordingly twofold: on the one hand the work of the intellect (*nous*) and the other, of the hand (*cheir*). These two aspects of the creative activity correspond to the "two in us" viz. our spiritual or intellectual Self and sensitive psychophysical Ego, working together (*synergo*). The integration of a work of art will depend upon the extent to which the Ego is able and willing to serve the Self or, if the patron and the workmen are two different persons, upon the measure of their mutual understanding.'[8]

The psychophysical self has to be purified in order to receive the reflection of Reality that contemplation generates and meditation reveals. It is this idea of detachment that Coleridge enunciated in his *Biographia Literaria* when he gave the example of the artist who failed to draw the image of perfect beauty because he had his wife as his model.[9]

When the writer does not believe in God and any higher norm, he feels the lack of it and then tries to concoct a norm or a world order himself, or depends on his partial realisation of Truth and gives that realisation the status of universality and totality and thereby falsifies the image of man. That is the difficulty that Twentieth century writers are faced with. Man has become disintegrated. That is why some important contemporary writers have tried to re-integrate man by reformulating their concepts and by establishing man's nature in a new context. That is what Ezra Pound, Yeats or D. H. Lawrence have tried to do. But the difficulty lies in the hidden style of these writers and their inability to see that they are trying to create various kinds of disconnected concepts. Their partial realisations are marred by their claim to have realised the whole.[10]

It is of course true that even those who are not fully aware of their own faith in the Divine Reality can create good literature provided they accept the basic conflict between good and evil presented in religion. It is from this moral framework of values that different writers receive sustenance. The genuineness and truthfulness of this realisation depends on the writer's acceptance of the framework. The acceptance of the framework is always at first an intellectual or a social habit. A writer goes on understanding emotionally the significance of this framework and making it a part of his self through the stress and strain of life where he has to take decisions and make choices.

Thus he grows and the morality grows within him. A great writer has the humanity to realise various possibilities and choices and the possibility of modified perceptions and realisations. Every moment is a new start. But only when there is a final goal and a supreme framework can this start indicate progress, achievement, expansion and realisation. Otherwise he may go round and round without any direction. Islam provides us with a final goal for man. No higher and greater goal has ever been conceived. With this goal in view and with the ethical code that enables man to practise and grow through knowledge and action, the writer can proceed towards a new destiny and ever new realisations.

III

Principles of Criticism and Methods of Teaching

Literature provides the best forum for training the sensibility of people; therefore the teaching of literature can be an effective means of making students realise the universality and absoluteness of certain values with reference to which writers study man and express their deeply felt understanding of life. This feeling and this realisation of truth is always a personal matter. The greatness of literature lies in the fact that the writer transcends personal limitations while presenting something of universal value. In other words, though his realisation is definitely personal, he is using himself as a means of going beyond the social and cultural environment and personal limitations into that region which may be regarded as universal and absolute. Even when the writer himself is a believer in a religion or in a dogma, he has to realise that this dogma or faith must be an experiential reality felt along the pulse and felt in the heart. Only then can it be a staple for poetry. Thus religious poetry can also become true poetry only when religion has turned into realisation, when the self of the poet has been able to emerge into a new state of consciousness after having dived deep into the eternity of the Absolute. That is how great religious poetry is born.

It is also possible to use the religious framework as a means of experiencing life and conditioning one's attitude to the facts of existence.

As Islam provides the Muslim world with such a framework, both this realisation and a religiously orientated attitude can easily find social validity. The problem, however, arises when society deviates from its basic religious mooring, and when this happens the reader cannot easily give his unconscious assent to that framework. The writer also becomes conscious of that lack of correspondence between himself and his reader and starts exploring his experiences in order to find a common language for artistic communication. He can easily draw on traditional experiences and use the symbolism inherent in images which are a common property of the society — images which Jung characterizes as 'archetypes'. But the dissociation of social sensibility brings about a lack of spiritual cohesion and the continually changing social conscience comes into conflict with the primordial tradition of one's culture. It is this conflict which drives the writer or the reader to find certainty, security and immortality within his own psyche or compels the writer to formulate his ideas and views in a deep personal cell. This is the problem of Western writers. Until now, however, this has not been a difficult problem in the Muslim world. Our society is still an integrated society. Although secularist forces are gradually gaining ascendancy in different parts of the Muslim world, although in some countries such as Turkey, Indonesia and Bangladesh the division between secularist and religious forces has led to open conflict, and although there is in each Muslim country a viable group educated according to the Western secular system of education, it is still possible to teach literature with reference to a basic norm of values derived from religion. It is the method of using this norm that we shall discuss here.

Literary Criticism and the Islamic Concept of Man

In order to teach literature effectively as literature and at the same time teach it as a means of the moral and spiritual training of students our basic need is for a scheme of literary criticism whose tenets are perfectly compatible with the concept of man which Islam provides. No writer can ever escape from his realisation, however unconscious that may be, of what man is. It is only when he tries to conceive man in his own way that he comes into conflict with religious ideals because his own realisation is bound to be extremely personal and hence limited. That is why it becomes necessary for literary critics to have a concept of good and evil. Basically it has never been difficult to have this concept, mainly because there is a universal recognition of certain values according to which man is judged. Islam has always claimed that there is only one religion in the universe, therefore, there has always been one basic universal code of morality, of good and evil. As literature is primarily concerned with human life on this earth, it is this universal code which the literary critic has to refer to in order to make students realise what is good literature and what is bad literature.

The problem arises when a writer dogmatises. When a writer is talking about love, sympathy, charity, mercy and their conflict with other forces as manifested in human situations, he is talking of things which appeal to all people of all ages. But when he tries to formulate a dogma on the basis of his experience he comes into conflict with other people's ideas. He is actually straying beyond the realm of pure literature into the realm of philosophical thought. Take the case of D. H. Lawrence, for example. His presentation of human characters and certain human situations has natural validity but the way in which he has presented them, the method with which he rouses the emotions and demands the assent of the reader to a scheme of life in which sex plays the most dominant and most effective role, make it difficult for the reader with religious feelings to accept this interpretation of life as something valid and true. What he has done is nothing but the generalisation of something extremely personal. This code is not entirely untrue, but it is highly partial, and because it is highly partial it becomes a dogma. He is theorising and therefore it is legitimate on the part of Muslim critics to point out to students how his realisation is extremely partial and hence his dogma about sex unjustified. There is of course great danger in this type of criticism being turned into a dogma of its own. One can, however, prevent that by keeping criticism within the context of literature in so far as a picture of human life and events is concerned.

We can take another example from a much greater writer — Shakespeare. If we take the play, *Romeo and Juliet*, we immediately notice that Shakespeare presents a conflict between good and evil but saves himself from dogmatisation by presenting love as both creative and destructive. Let us take the last event, the two suicides — Romeo drinking poison and dying and Juliet killing herself. From the manner of presentation it is obvious that our sympathy is aroused and we do not condemn Romeo and Juliet for sinning, though they have committed suicide. In fact, we feel that they have proved beyond doubt the complete achievement of selflessness through love. Is this attitude generated by Shakespeare towards these lovers anti-religious? It could have been treated as anti-religious had Shakespeare evoked in the minds of the readers and the spectators an admiration for the principle of suicide. He does not do so. On the other hand, he presents it as a tragic waste of two young lives because of forces beyond their control. Whereas love should be creative and joy-giving, prevention of the consummation of love has led to this frustration and disaster. Thus Shakespeare's picture is highly compatible with the religious concept of life.

Even if we take a more difficult play *Anthony and Cleopatra*, we find that there also Shakespeare is not essentially anti-religious as Wimsatt has tried to prove. It is true that he has presented what could be considered adulterous love as something which seems to ennoble and glorify both the lover and the beloved. But even when Cleopatra seems to have gone beyond narrow selfish limits and expanded into a great lover, the reader has a feeling that neither Anthony nor Cleopatra has purity in their love. There seems to be a Hegelian conflict between right and wrong, between duty and love. Shakespeare has also presented this love as a destructive force and not as a power that ennobles and strengthens the spirit of either Anthony or Cleopatra. The defeat of Anthony in the battle is presented in such a manner that the reader and the spectator condemn both Anthony and Cleopatra for their folly. They never feel that the sacrifice of honour to love by Anthony is a highly praiseworthy thing. Rather, the feeling that is generated is one of tragic waste. Cleopatra is nowhere presented as a selfless lover. Her love for Anthony is always mixed with extreme selfishness. Therefore, when discussing *Anthony and Cleopatra* the teacher does not have to bring in his religious dogma in order to show that the conflict between good and evil is something unacceptable. The human situation presented by Shakespeare is compatible with religious feeling. It is a feeling of the great tragic waste of human potentiality through a form of love which has not transcended selfish limits.

It is possible, therefore, to teach all kinds of literature without disturbing or opposing religious attitudes and feelings, provided the teacher indicates to the students how the writer is confined or not confined within the range of normal human experience, how values invoked by the writer are not highly occult, personal and dogmatic. The teacher is justified in making students realise that literature can be condemned only when the writer strays beyond the limits of a natural and normal realisation of truth through human experience into the region of philosophy and dogma where he uses literature as a means of conveying a philosophy and a way of life which a religious man may not accept. The reader may willingly go with the writer and suspend his disbelief only to be able to respond to the human situations presented by the writer. When the writer tries to propagate a philosophy he should be criticised from the extra-literary point of view, which is the point of view of a thinker.

Is Literature Independent of Morals and Religion?

The question, of course, arises as to how far the teacher can go and whether by presenting these situations the teacher is not using his own dogma to criticise literature. Here the question of complete independence of literature arises. Is literature such a discipline that it should be regarded as something beyond the pale of all moral and social codes of life? Is its realisation of Truth so sacred that all other truths have to be forgotten, the code of life suspended and all value judgments ignored, in order to appreciate it? One may not agree with this particular concept of literature. If one has to give complete independence to literature, independence from all social, moral and spiritual laws, then one has to give the same independence to natural and social sciences and in fact to all other branches of human knowledge. Each branch of human knowledge becomes thus an independent separate entity, without any coherence and transcendental unity. This attitude leads to the disintegration of human personality which has taken place in the West. The Islamic concept of man is presented to us in the Holy Qurān and the *Sunnah* as the concept of an integrated personality governed by transcendental laws, transcendental in the sense that the laws and the code of life are based on absolute values. Hence all partial realisation of those values by individuals or societies in any particular period of time cannot be regarded as complete and perfect. Human culture is integrally tied up with these absolute values, but the emphasis on certain values in a particular period of time depends on the changing environment. This change in environment comes through man's application of knowledge to life. This process has been going on from the time of Adam and Eve, and will continue to the end of the world. As a result man is continually evolving new instruments of civilization and these are changing the social environment of individuals and societies. But basic cultural values have remained unchanged. The greatness of literature depends on its ability to penetrate beyond changing environments into the basic problems of life relevant to the absolutes that form the primordial traditions of man. When a writer is not bogged down by the superficialities of external circumstances and is able to understand the human problem, or rather the problem of man's adherence to basic values in the context of new situations, then he has penetrated into a reality which will appeal to later generations. It is this ability that enabled Aeschylus, Sophocles, Homer, Firdawsi or the Noh playwrights of Japan to present those situations to us which we in the twentieth century can appreciate and respond to:

The Teacher as Critic

The teacher of literature must therefore play the role of the critic. He has to discern the depth of writings according to the ability of the authors to go beyond the superficial, the social and individual circumstances and penetrate into the realms of reality. He has to remove the temporary garments of personal prejudices, occult dogmas and partial metaphysics and see naked truth about humanity. No writer can have a complete knowledge of this truth; hence no critic can claim such completeness for anyone. Nor can a writer demand that his dogma or metaphysics be accepted by all readers. As a critic the teacher has to see how far occult dogmas or wrongly understood metaphysics are colouring the vision of the writer; how far the writer's emotive response to the human situation is governed by his day to day conventions and customs; and how far the writer has succeeded in concentrating his attention on essential, universal human problems which are surrounded by socio-cultural accretions or which have their peculiar slant and complexity because of contemporary socio-cultural conditions.

The Teacher as a Religious Leader

The dual rôle of teacher and religious leader can be achieved only when the critic (or the teacher) has a sensitive soul and has realised what true humanity means. Islam teaches this to him through its prescribed code of life. But only when he practises it himself can this human perspective and its attendant problems become a matter of self-realisation. That is why only a practising Muslim can have that broad sympathetic soul that is aware of human limitations, evil temptations and human greatness. Unless a teacher has that breadth of vision, depth of realisation and the supreme ideal of human nobility and greatness enshrined in the concept of man as the vice-gerent (*khalīfatullāh*) of God he cannot be a good critic, nor is his perceptive ability discriminating enough to sift the experiences presented in literature.

As literature presents life as experienced and realised by individual writers, it cannot be treated as something entirely independent or even partially outside the scope of what we understand by the word 'humanity'. And as Islam gives us the noblest concept of humanity and shows us the way of life that enables us to reach that zenith, and also the other way that leads to self-destruction, we have a basic norm providing us with criteria about right and wrong, good and evil. A teacher imbibes this norm and is expected to uphold it almost unconsciously. The more conscious he becomes of the norm the more minutely can he judge himself and make that norm prevail among children. Muslim children are expected to absorb this norm and these fundamental assumptions about man's duties and responsibilities as a servant of God and hence as a man in the home, in school, in society and in nature. These are basic assumptions that will provide the critic (or the teacher) with standards with which he will be able to measure the extent of a writer's response to life as presented in his literature. They will also help him to evaluate the writer's range and special variety, and his typically individual way of responding to human situations enshrined in literature.

The great danger lies in treating this norm as a series of institutionalised formulae and applying them without reference to the complexity of human choice and human freedom. The norm provided by Islam is the highest and most universal conceivable for mankind. But the moment this norm gets an institutionalised form it becomes confined to a code applicable for Muslims only. Moreover, since institutions change in the course of time, it is not the institutionalised form of the code that the critic should apply, but the fundamentals on the basis of which institutions go on growing, changing or flourishing. Extramarital love for example may lead someone to have an adulterous relationship. If this is presented as a desirable thing, it should be condemned as advocating an undesirable norm. But it can be presented as a source of conflict in the minds of the hero and heroine. Here the writer's attitude would be that of a human being who has accepted the basic assumptions of that code.

If the teacher, on the other hand, takes a permissive attitude and is tolerant of a writer whose code of life is completely at variance with the Islamic code thus leaving students in a vacuum and allowing them to respond to the writing or be influenced by it as they like, he will not be doing justice either to literature or to students. Literature can be extremely seductive and may even be misleading, corroding and destructive. Professor Hoggart has very effectively demonstrated this point in *Uses of Literacy*. That is why literature can be used as a propaganda machine. The teacher has to train the sensibility of students is such a manner that they do not succumb to such propaganda but always evaluate the genuiness of the human condition with reference to the absolute norm of human conduct. A typical Communist writer for example invariably presents a rich man or a capitalist as a corrupt person. That means that he is presenting a type conceived by him and not found invariably in any society. A human being refers unconsciously to a norm which is superior to the day-to-day changing social norm whenever a basic human problem arises. His humanity is superior to capitalism or socialism. Islam asserts that 'human' norm which is divinely sanctioned.

Choosing Literature for the Curriculum

The stand, therefore, the teacher can legitimately take is that of a person who accepts man's responsibility for his actions, but who at the same time realises that there are various forces at work — forces which the Holy Quran presents as the forces of Satan and the forces of self. It is only when the teacher takes that stand that he can select standard literary works and analyse motivations and situations with reference to the complex condition of human life. This complex condition has been variously interpreted by modern psychologists and sociologists but some times they almost make man completely dependent on external forces or internal forces beyond man's control. Here lies the greatness and naturalness of the Islamic concept which presents man as potentially capable of reaching the Truth because God has breathed His own Spirit in man. But at the same time he is surrounded by forces which distract him from the path of Truth. Literature can thus be taught as an individual writer's various perceptions of this truth about man. This perception is obviously partial and individual, although it is always the attempt of the writer to universalise that perception. Because of this variety of moral perceptions, it is necessary for the teacher to consider the fact that no writer has attained the complete truth about everything in life. Therefore, the choice of texts to be studied by a class of students ought to be varied. But at the same time the teacher ought to concentrate on a few standard works which present different kinds of perception and different views of life. He should be able to indicate moral deficiencies in old and new literature, and even great literature, and never take the attitude that all great literature and art is unequivocally complete and humanitarian from the Islamic point of view. At the same time he should demonstrate how different writers may have seen different aspects of human personality. That is why it has not been possible for the same writer to capture the interest of succeeding generations. This particular statement of course assumes that man is eternally the same but because of social and circumstantial differences in the journey of life different aspects of human personality are emphasised in different periods of human history. In framing the curriculum, therefore, the teacher should not be guided by the judgment of contemporary critics only. He should be detached enough to have an overall view of the entire growth of literature and choose masterpieces as well as important period pieces so as to enable students to become acquainted with the variety and depth of literature.

The next important principle to be kept in view in choosing literary works for classroom study is the variety of effects. This is of course a usual and normal principle followed everywhere since a pattern has been evolved and is now accepted in all countries. This pattern indicates effects known as tragic, comic, farcical or serious, light, folk or just entertainment. Each of these effects is integrally related to a moral principle. This becomes clear when we read Aristotle's analysis of the tragic effect of pity and terror. It is by analysing these effects and their relationship to the type of characters and human situations presented by the writer that the teacher may train not merely the artistic sensibility of students but also their moral sensibility. This of course does not mean that literary effect is the same as moral effect but it definitely indicates that moral judgments enter into our literary judgments. Therefore, while responding to tragic feelings aroused by incidents and situations in a play like *King Lear*, we are bringing our moral judgment into operation because our appreciation of King Lear's misery and suffering is integrally tied up with our condemnation of the attitudes and behaviour of Goneril and Regan. Even when we look at the bewilderment and lack of moral conclusions in such plays as those of Harold Pinter, our assumptions are moral assumptions derived from our basic training as human beings. If we find that there is confusion and a loss of direction, we understand that they are undesirable elements of life. Thus the teacher is expected to make students conscious of the loss of direction that this type of modern literature presents to us. Even if literature of poor quality is presented to them, the teacher should indicate the reasons for its low quality. Thus, here again, the choice of literature and the method of teaching are both integrally related to the moral framework of life.

Islam as a Frame of Reference

The works of literature cannot by themselves provide a moral framework for exploration. Literature is not completely independent of life. The only independence that it can claim from the moral point of view is the independence that the writer can claim for himself. By simply stating that each writer's vision of life is unique, the writer cannot claim complete isolation from the framework of life within which he exists. Therefore, his independence lies in claiming a personal realisation of Truth and in the mode of presenting that realisation through literature. This realisation is partial and not total, but in order to appreciate it sympathetically we may have to suspend our personal judgments temporarily and identify ourselves with those living in the writer's world created in that work of art; but that particular realisation of ours has to be judged by placing it in the context of the total vision of life provided in God-given concepts.

In other words, there is always a referential framework and it becomes necessary that the writer, as a human being, who does not want to be influenced by all kinds of attitudes and who does not want to be moved in different directions by different writers, should evaluate the moral framework which he believes in and which provides complete guidance to the reader. As a religious person, a Muslim believes that every kind of knowledge except divine knowledge remains partial and that a realisation of this has led man towards the realisation of his relationship with God. However sympathetic he may be towards a writer like D. H. Lawrence, J. Conrad, W. B. Yeats or Maxim Gorki, he cannot accept their moral frameworks as something beyond the judgment of the individual. He cannot at the same time consider their findings as ultimate and irrefutable and hence completely acceptable. All that he can do is give the writer credit for the truth that writer presents about human nature, human motives and the variety of human situations. The best method that the teacher can adopt in order to save students from being influenced by one author or another is to make students study the works of different writers who are at variance with each other. The teacher and students can then objectively explore the moral frameworks of different writers and find how conflicting their judgments and realisations are. At the same time this will be a highly instructive exploration for students if they are trying to find out how, in spite of the variety of realisations, these writers have been able to present truthful images about man in various situations.

If this comparative method is followed, then literature can be used as a means of understanding and appreciating human motivation and emotion. The teacher can then focus his attention on the concept of character, indicating the complexities of human life through the complexities of human motivations. Students will also be able to study characters at different levels of sophistication. This exploration has to retain its objectivity if the teacher wants students to understand the unique and original interpretation of life offered by each writer. Through comparison and contrast they will understand the variety, as well as judge the quality, range and depth of perception, of the writing. It is through these explorations of various characters presented by writers that the teacher can make students aware of the problems of understanding human nature. The same would be true of the exploration of human situations presented by writers. While trying to ascertain the emotions involved in these situations the teacher can lead students beyond the temporary causes of these emotions to eternal causes, and indicate the universality of human problems. Since literature can be treated as a collection of specific examples of human situations and motivations, it will be possible for students to appreciate both the universality of moral dilemmas faced by human beings and the form these dilemmas take in specific human situations in different countries and different ages.

Literature and the Feelings

But literature should be treated as literature and not as a substitute for moral teaching. Literature can never replace morality or religion. One of the basic functions of literature is to provide enjoyment. Even when one is presenting a tragic situation it must ultimately be enjoyable. Only then can it transcend the bitterness of actual situations and be transformed into what we know as literature. Kant studies the character of feelings roused by literature and finds that the reader's feelings are aesthetic in character, leading to contemplative consciousness and not to actual action. When Othello is killing Desdemona we do not rush to the stage to prevent him from doing wrong, though we would have done so had a friend of ours been doing exactly the same thing in actual life and had we known he was doing something so foolish and wrong. We, on the other hand, contemplate on the situation presented by that scene.

Our feelings are thus divorced from moral action when we try to appreciate literature. It is, at the same time, not divorced from moral perception or moral contemplation. The pleasure that we get is derived from our realisation of such human conditions and from our appreciation of the method of presenting this situation through artistic means. It is necessary, therefore, for the teacher to help students realise this condition and save them from making overt moral judgments on any human situation presented in literature. The total framework of life taught by Islam should enable them to see the limitations of the writer and appreciate the limited framework within which the writer is exploring human consciousness; but the typical artistic transformation of ordinary emotions into aesthetic emotions could help the reader to attain a state of detachment which would enable him to contemplate emotions, motivations and human situations. Although the teacher has to keep in view the total framework of life and evaluate the moral framework presented by the writer and judge the merit or otherwise of the writer's individual framework, it is necessary for him to train the sensibility of students so that they can correctly and adequately contemplate emotions and feelings aroused by a work of art. The teacher's function, therefore, is not to settle all morally critical questions in advance. He has to make a selection of works which will provide apt contrasts in moral sensibilities and ensure free and frank discussion on the sensibilities they embody. The teacher's own moral judgment and training will obviously influence these discussions.

IV

Conclusions and Recommendations

1. To teach literature effectively the first requirement is an awareness of the place of literature in the total scheme of knowledge. This means that the total scheme of knowledge has to be classified from the Islamic point of view.
2. The next important factor is a proper school of literacy criticism which can establish an integral relationship between good literature and the religious concept of values but at the same time, indicate the independence of literature within the framework of those values. This would mean establishing a relationship between the total scheme of values stated earlier and the different aspects of human personality and the different functions that man can legitimately perform within the context of an overall scheme of life.
3. Teachers, therefore, need to be properly trained. They should be responsive, their moral sensitivity should be adequately developed from the religious point of view so that they have mastery of themselves within the moral framework of their lives, and they should have a sensitive soul ready to respond to the sentiments expressed in literature. A teacher should also be well versed in the artistic conventions of literature, i.e. those of the forms, rules, regulations, myths, images and symbols in all basic literary traditions, so as to be able to give students appropriate tools for analysis and comprehension. He should also be fluent in the language in which that literature is written so that he can grasp fully the implications of meanings, the exactitude of words, phrases and sentences and the precision or otherwise of the creative mind behind the linguistic

facade. Thus will he be able to analyse, appreciate and evaluate the organisation of the mind and the range and depth of creativity of the writer. He will then be in a position to discipline the minds of his students and teach them how to gauge the range and depth of perception of life expressed in the works they study.

4. As it is not possible to prevent students from reading bad literature if it is available and from being influenced by modern life which is becoming increasingly secularised and detached from the religious scheme of values, it is necessary to include in the curriculum for detailed study only those works which are recognised as classics because of their deeper and wider understanding of humanity and also because of the deep moral framework of life portrayed by the writer. At the same time the teacher should compare and contrast such works with those of inferior quality so as to enable students to appreciate the difference and to learn how to differentiate good and bad literature.

5. Great literature is that kind of creative work which upholds and establishes those universal values of life which man has learnt from religion, literature which is so natural and rational that it is appreciated and accepted by people of all ages and regions. The differences in individual perception are due to the differences in quality, range and depth of individual realisations of Truth. These realisations are not arrived at through logic, argument or rational thought, but through an appeal to man's own humanity and his deeper self. It is essential for teachers to be able to make this literary sensibility penetrating and strong, and integrally related with man's moral sensibility so that a student's own inner self becomes a bulwark against the evils of life.

6. The above statements do not mean that the teacher should in any way impose himself upon students and be dogmatic in his evaluations and judgements. He, on the contrary, should train students to be sufficiently detached to see the point of view of the writer, his vision of life and moral depth, without being completely swept away from their own moorings. In other words, the literary sensibility must be aesthetic enough to enable the reader to appreciate the quality of life the author presents. Students must learn, therefore, to raise their sights and appreciate the peculiar or special feelings generated by a particular work of art. At the same time this detachment should not create a sense of neutrality in students, because they must be able to retain their own religious convictions, so that after appreciating the different points of view of various writers, they can compare, contrast and evaluate their comparative merits.

7. It is also evident from the above discussions that the training of literary sensibility ought to be related to ethical education. Unless a student

grows up as a true Muslim he will not be able to relate aesthetic education to ethics. If by aesthetic education is meant the development of the ability to perceive fully and understand adequately the beautiful and its meaning in the arts, it needs to be complemented by ethical education so that the relationship between the good and the beautiful is felt and appreciated. This is only possible when the beautiful is understood to be a manifestation of the great principle of Beauty, which is nothing less than an attribute of God. Only then does one find Beauty and morality integrated in a common framework of life. The variations in aesthetic judgements are the results of the different emphases that are placed on different aspects of human personality in different ages. This difference in emphasis is due to changes in social and historical conditions brought about by the instruments of civilisation. Otherwise man is eternally and universally the same creature.

8. In order that aesthetic education may become part and parcel of the education of the total personality of a Muslim it is necessary to strike a balance between spiritual, rational and aesthetic perceptions. Only by understanding how Truth and Beauty are but Attributes of God can this balance be struck. We will only create a disintegrated personality if we assert that there is such a thing as 'pure sensation' or 'pure thinking' or 'pure aesthetic' perception. As Truth and Beauty are the Attributes of God and as this entire creation is nothing but the manifestation of all the Qualities and Powers of God, in other words, the Attributes of God, the reflection in art of this Beauty and Truth is nothing but a reflection of the beautiful in life. Thus aesthetics connects the teaching of the beautiful in the arts with the teaching of ethics. It is therefore necessary for every teacher to have a firm grounding in the values of life so that he himself can grow up as a true servant of God. Only then can he rear our youth in the spirit and greatness of man and also instil in them an abhorrence of the evils of materialism and of the limitation of so-called humanism.

9. In order for the above aims and objectives of teaching literature to be achieved it is further necessary to devise courses in both language and literature so that the moral upbringing of the student and the training of his aesthetic sensibility can be integrated into a comprehensive religious scheme of life. At the same time the student should grow up as a person who loves his independence, and whose individual perception of reality is not threatened by the imposition of dogmas. As literature is a very powerful weapon, from the very beginning of school life a whole programme of courses in literature and history and other social sciences should be so integrated that the student attains a comprehensive view of life from the material he reads and through the method in which he is

trained. A detailed programme of study of such an integrated course needs to be carefully planned.

NOTES

1. al-Qurān, XV, 29.
2. *Ibid.*, II, 31.
3. *Ibid.*, XCV, 4.
4. *Ibid.*, XV, 29.
5. *Ibid.*, XII, 53.

Three stages and levels of the development of the human soul have been envisaged in the Qurān. The lowest stage of the soul is called *al-nafs al-ammārah*, a stage in which the soul or mind is controlled by the desires and passions and is prone to evil, and if not checked and controlled, will lead man to moral and spiritual ruin. The second stage is known as *al-nafs al-lawwāmah* (Qurān, Lxxv; 2) or self-reproaching soul or self—in conflict between good and evil. At this stage quite often the 'intellect' frees itself from spiritual domination and creates a conflict between spiritual demand and the demands of the lower self but because of its awareness of evil, the soul saves itself through penitence and God's mercy. The third stage is that of *al-nafs al-mutma' innah* (Qurān LXXXIX; 27)—the purified soul in which the intellect willingly and happily accepts the dominance of the spirit and the spirit of man keeps all passions and desires under legitimate control. Only then can man be at peace with himself and with the rest of the world and look on life and death, suffering and joy with complete detachment. Ghazzāli discusses these stages lucidly and in detail from the psychological point of view in *Ihyā' 'ulūm al-dīn* (Arabic) and *Kimiyā-ye sa'ādat* (Persian). Islam believes that from the first man there has been only one religion and hence the same basic concept of man prevails in different cultures and civilizations in spite of ramifications and additions and alterations by later adherents. Thus there is a perennial or primordial tradition permeating diverse cultures. See the concept of *Tamo, Rajo* and *Satto* in Hindu mysticism. *Atma-Bodha* in René Guénon, *Introduction to the study of the Hindu Doctrines*, London, 1945, and Patañjali's doctrines in Swami Prabhananda and C. Isherwood, eds. *How to Know God: The Yoga Aphorisms of Patanjali*, New York, 1953. See also J. Mascare (trans.), *Himalayas of the Soul; Translations from the Sanskrit of the Principal Uponishadas*, London, 1945. See also Ananda Koomaraswamy for his treatment of the problem of the nature and the final end of man, especially the following: 'Who is "Satan" and where is "Hell"?', 'On Being in One's Right Mind.', *Spiritual Authority and Temporal Power in the Indian Theory of Government*; 'Akimcanna: self-naughting.' 'The Indian Doctrine of Man's Last End'; *Hinduism and Buddhism*; and 'Recollection, Indian and Platonic.' See also J. Pieper, *The Human Wisdom of St. Thomas*, New York, 1948.

6. Qurān, xcv; 5.
7. *Ibid.*, xv, 31–44. Satan has no authority over totally dedicated believers but he can mislead others. Satan says; 'I will put them all in the wrong except Thy servants among them, sincere and purified (by Thy grace)' (Qurān xv; 39).
8. 'Athena and Hephaistan', *Journal of Indian Society of Oriental Art, Vol. xv*.
9. Chapter XV.
10. The most severe indictment of these three authors was made by T. S. Eliot in *After Strange Gods*.

Chapter Three

The Rôle of Fine Arts in Muslim Education

Ibrahim Titus Burckhardt

Born 1908, Florence; since childhood strongly attracted to oriental art which led him to an intense study of eastern doctrines and to repeated sojourns in Islamic countries; embraced Islam in 1934 while in Fez, Morocco; from 1941 to 1968 directed a publishing house in Switzerland and specialised in the edition of ancient manuscripts; since 1972 working as an expert of UNESCO for the preservation of the cultural legacy of Fez; publications include: *Art of Islam, Language and Meaning*, (London, 1976), *An Introduction to Sufi Doctrine* (Lahore, 1959, Wellingborough, 1976); *Moorish Culture in Spain* (London, 1972), *Sacred Art in East and West*, (London 1967).

Let us first consider the place Islamic art occupies in modern academic teaching, for it is through that teaching and more exactly through the two disciplines of archaeology and history of art that many Muslim students approach the artistic legacy of Islam. Archaeology and the history of art are two branches of one science, born in Eighteenth century Europe as a sister to humanistic philosophy, an agnostic philosophy which reduces all spiritual values to their purely human aspect. One may therefore ask whether this science, which has incontestably accumulated a great deal of valuable data as well as contributed to the preservation of many precious monuments, is able to understand, not only the outward history of Islamic art, but also its spiritutal content.

Archaeology and the history of art are both founded on the historical analysis of works of art. Such analysis may well deliver objective results but it does not necessarily lead to an essential view of things. On the contrary it has a tendency to stop at details at the expense of more comprehensive views, just as if a man looking at a wall built with stones tried to understand the very reason for the existence of that wall by tracing back each single stone to its origin. This is exactly what has happened with many scholars who have tried to explain the origin of Islamic art by tracing back every element of Islamic art to some precedent in Byzantine, Sassanid, Coptic or other art. They have lost sight of the intrinsic and original unity of Islamic art. They have forgotten the seal which Islam put upon all those borrowed elements.

It is true that the history of art received many new impulses through the study of the art of oriental civilizations. However, it has not easily freed itself from certain prejudices stemming from its very origin, the most deeply rooted of these prejudices being the habit of judging the value of a work of art by the degree of its real or presumed 'originality' or by virtue of its 'revolutionary' character, as if the essential quality of a work of art were not its beauty, and as if beauty were not independent of the psychological dramas of the moment. But most historians of art are primarily interested in the individuality of the artist; they are not directly concerned with the spiritual truth which an art may convey. What they try to capture is the psychological impulse which has led to such or such an artistic expression. Now this individualism or psychologism, as we may call it, is as far as possible from the spirit of Islamic art which never became the stage of individual problems and experiences. The Muslim artist, by his very *Islam*, his surrender to the Divine Law, is always aware of the fact that it is not he who produces or invents beauty, but that a work of art is beautiful to the degree it obeys the cosmic order and therefore reflects universal beauty: *Al-ḥamdu li'llāh waḥdah*. This awareness, if it excludes Promethean attitudes, by no means diminishes the joy of artistic creativity, as the works themselves testify. Rather, it confers on Islamic art a serene and somehow impersonal character. For the Muslim mind art reminds man of God when it is as impersonal as the laws which govern the movement of the heavenly spheres.

For modern 'psychologism' therefore Islamic art is a closed book, even more so as it hardly offers anything analogous to the representation of human beings, as one finds in European art. In Western civilization, influenced as it is by Greek art as well as by Christian iconography, the image of man occupies the central position of all visual art, whereas in the world of Islam the image of man plays a secondary rôle and is altogether absent from the liturgical domain. As you may well know, the Islamic negation of anthropomorphic art is both absolute and conditional: it is absolute with regard to all images which could be an object of worship, and it is conditional with regard to art forms imitating living bodies. We refer to the saying of the Blessed Prophet who condemned artists who try to 'ape' the creation of God: in their afterlife they will be ordered to give life to their works and will suffer from their incapacity to do so. This *ḥadīth* has been interpreted in different ways. In general, it was understood as the condemnation of an intrinsically blasphemous intention, and therefore Islam tolerates anthropomorphic art forms on the condition that they do not create the illusion of living beings. In miniature painting, for instance, central perspective suggesting three-dimensional space has been avoided.

From the European point of view the Islamic restriction on figurative art seems excessive. It is responsible, as has been asserted, for cultural impoverishment. The history of European art, however, fully justifies the Islamic 'aniconism'. European religious art, as it developed since the Middle Ages, or more exactly since the naturalistic trend of the Renaissance, strongly contributed to rob religion of its credibility.

And let us not forget that the image of man is always the image man conceives of himself. The image reacts against its author, who thus never quite frees himself from the spell his image casts on him. The whole evolution of European art with its increasingly accelerated phases of action and reaction is mainly a dialogue between man and his image. Islam banished all this ambiguous play of psychological mirrors at an earlier stage, thus preserving the primordial dignity of man himself.

The European conception of art and its conception in the world of Islam are different to the point that one may ask whether the common use of such words as 'art' and 'artist' does not create more confusion than mutual understanding. Almost everything in European art is image. Consequently the highest rank in the hierarchy of European art is held by figurative painting and sculpture. These are 'free arts', whereas architecture as conditioned by technical necessities occupies a lower rank. Even 'lower' are the 'decorative' arts. From the European point of view, the criterion of an artistic culture lies in its capacity to represent nature and even more in its capacity to portray man. From the Islamic point of view, on the contrary, the main scope of art is not imitation or description of nature — man's work will never equal God's art — but the shaping of human ambience. Art has to endow all objects by which man naturally surrounds himself — a house, a fountain, a drinking vessel, a garment, a carpet — with the perfection each object can possess according to its own nature. The perfection of a building for instance, stems from three-dimensional geometry according to the perfection of the crystalline state of matter, while the art of the carpet involves two dimensional geometry as well as the harmony of colours. Islamic art does not add something alien to the objects it shapes; it only brings forth their potential qualities. It is essentially objective; in fact, neither the research of the most perfect profile for a cupola nor the rhythmical display of a linear ornament have much to do with the personal mood of the artist. The central theme of European art — and we might also say the central theme of Christian art — is the image of man. In Islam too, man is the centre to which all arts refer, but as a rule he is not himself a theme of visual art. If we consider the general Islamic resistance against figurative art or against anthropomorphic art in all its depth, we discover a tremendous respect for the

Divine Origin of human form. The same is true, in a way, for traditional Christian art, but the consequences, on both sides, are entirely different.

Here we ought to trace a sketch of the hierarchy of visual arts in the world of Islam. The most noble of all its arts is the art of writing or calligraphy, for this has the privilege of translating into visual forms the divine speech of the Holy Qurān. Indeed, Arabic calligraphy has not only reached the highest perfection; it also has brought forth a wide scale of different styles from the purely static rectangular *kūfī* to the most fluid and melodious forms of *naskhī*. Wherever Islam has reigned, the jewels of Arabic calligraphy are scattered.

Almost as important is the art of architecture. One can say that it occupies the central position among all those arts that shape the human ambience and make it akin to the Islamic *barakah*. Most of the minor arts like wood carving, mosaics, sculpture and so on are attached to architecture. We call them 'minor arts' according to the conventional terminology, but in fact they never occupied a lower rank in the Muslim world. This fact is true of even the so-called utilitarian arts, for they partake of the dignity of man as the 'representative of God on earth.'

Before the world of Islam was invaded by the products of modern industry, no object came out of the hands of a Muslim craftsman without being endowed with some beauty, whether it was a building or a domestic implement, whether it was made for a rich or a poor customer. The material used by the craftsman might be humble and his instruments very simple; his work was nonetheless noble. The reason for this remarkable fact is that beauty is inherent in Islam itself; it flows from its innermost reality, which is Unity (*al-tawḥīd*) manifesting itself as justice (*'adl*) and generosity (*karam*). Unity, justice and generosity are three qualities that are also three aspects of beauty and almost its definition, as will be more apparent if we call them unity, equilibrium and plenitude. At the level of art, justice becomes equilibrium and generosity becomes plenitude, whereas unity is the common source of all perfections.

If we consider inner beauty and outward beauty we find that the latter comes from the former. To the extent that human activities are integrated into Islam, they become a support for beauty — a beauty which in fact transcends those activities because it is the beauty of Islam. Not only is this true of the fine arts, it holds true for them in a more direct fashion as it is their rôle to manifest the hidden qualities of things. The art of Islam receives its beauty not from any ethnic genius but from Islam itself.

The beauty of the arts of Islam — we might also say the beauty that Islam normally conveys to its surroundings — is like a silent teaching which helps and deepens the doctrinal teaching transmitted by religious education. It penetrates into the soul without passing through rational thought. For many believers it is a more direct argument than pure doctrine. It is like the life or the flesh of religion whilst theology, law and ethics are its skeleton.

For this reason the existence of art is a vital necessity in the spiritual and social economy of Islam. Art, however, cannot exist without the artist or without the craftsman, no distinction being made between the two in the traditional world of Islam where an art without craftsmanship or a technical achievement without beauty are both inconceivable. This means that the gradual withdrawal of the crafts as a result of the inroads of the machine entails the partial or total disappearance of the Islamic arts. At once religious education is robbed of at least two of its supports, namely the silent aid of an all-pervading beauty — there are still some traces left, but for how long? — and the more direct help of the professional activities (in the crafts) normally oriented towards a spiritual aim.

Professional education (in the crafts) converges with spiritual teaching wherever it strives towards that kind of perfection which the Blessed Prophet meant in saying, 'God prescribes perfection in all things' (*kataba 'Llāhu iḥsāna 'alā kulli shay*'). The word *iḥsān*, translated by 'perfection', means also 'beauty' and 'virtue'; more exactly it means the inner beauty, the beauty of the soul or the heart which necessarily emanates outwards transforming every human activity into an art and every art into a remembrance of God (*dhikrallāh*).

There is no Muslim artist who has not inherited from his predecessors. If he should disregard the models tradition offers him, he would soon prove his ignorance of their intrinsic meaning and spiritual value; being ignorant of that, he could not put his heart into those forms. Instead of tradition there would only be sterile repetition. This is exactly the phenomenon for which certain European scholars reproach Islamic art. They argue that this art gradually died from lack of imagination. But in fact the arts of Islam never lost their inner substance until modern industry dealt them a deadly blow. The arts of Islam have died because their very foundations, the traditional crafts, have been destroyed.

Yet, not all the traditional crafts and arts have disappeared; in some places they survive, and all efforts should be made to protect them, for industrialization is not the real solution to all social problems. We have considered the place Islamic art occupies in modern academic teaching as well as in the assessment of traditional crafts. Incidentally we have shown that Islamic art is not only the art of Muslim peoples, but is deeply rooted in the spirit of Islam itself. Whoever wishes to have a more detailed demonstration of this fact, will find it in my book *The Art of Islam* published in 1976 in London. There is no doubt that not only do the various forms of Islamic art have common features, but that its variety is in itself a manifestation of an essential unity, just like the variations of a single theme in traditional music.

We may now resume our main subject and ask the question whether a knowledge of Islamic art is vital to Muslim education. If we simplify the question and put it in the following words: 'Is Islamic art vital to Islam itself?', every Muslim, I presume, will answer 'No'. Islam as a path to Divine Truth does not depend on any cultural circumstances; a Bedouin may be as perfect a Muslim as a scholar, and a simple *muṣallā* in the desert surrounded by a line of stones with a bigger stone indicating the direction of the *Ka'bah* can be as valuable a prayer place as the Pearl Mosque in Delhi. Cultural development is not necessarily identical with spiritual achievement. Let us then ask: 'Can a Muslim community live within a cultural framework alien to Islam? Experience shows that it can survive but not prosper. But our question probably will call forth the remark that a cultural framework involves diffferent elements of a more or less influential character, materialistic philosophy and sociology being certainly a greater handicap to Muslim education than the experience of non-Islamic art or rather than the absence of Islamic art. For art deals with appearance whereas philosophy or psychology touches the heart of things. This judgement, however, is one-sided; it forgets that art, while dealing in fact with the exterior aspect of things, at the same time reveals an interior dimension of reality.

The essence of art is beauty, and beauty is by its very nature an exterior as well as an interior reality. According to a well-known saying of the Blessed Prophet, 'God is beautiful and He loves beauty' (*Allāhu jamīlun yuhibbu' l-jamāl*). Beauty therefore is a Divine Quality (*ṣifah ilāhiyyah*) reflected in whatsoever is beautiful on earth. Some scholars perhaps will object that beauty mentioned in the *hadīth* is of a purely moral character, but there is no reason why we should limit the import of this prophetical word, nor why Divine Beauty should not shine forth at every level of existence. No doubt Divine Beauty is incomparably exalted above physical as well as above moral beauty, but at the same time nothing beautiful can exist outside the dominion of that Divine Quality. 'God is beautiful and He loves beauty'; this means that He loves His own reflection in the world.

According to a number of famous Muslim metaphysicians, Divine Beauty (*jamāl*) includes all the Divine Attributes expressing bounty and grace or the merciful irradiation of God in the world, whereas Divine

Majesty (*jalāl*) includes all the Divine Attributes of severity, which in a way manifests the transcendant nature of God with regard to His creation. More generally speaking, each Divine Quality contains all the others, for they all refer to one single Essence. Therefore beauty implies truth (*ḥaqq*) and vice-versa: truth implies beauty. There is no real beauty which does not have truth concealed in it, and there is no real truth from which beauty does not emanate. This reciprocal character of universal qualities has its reflection at the level of traditional teaching, and in this connection it has been said: 'In Islam art is a science and science is an art.' These words refer directly to the geometrical lore involved in Islamic art, a lore which allows the artist to develop harmonious forms from fundamental geometrical patterns. According to a higher level of meaning, however, art is a science because it opens up a way of contemplative knowledge whose ultimate object is Divine Beauty, and science is an art insofar as it is oriented towards unity and therefore possesses a sense of equilibrium or harmony which lends it a kind of beauty.

Modern European art, whatever beauty it may occasionally offer, is generally enclosed within the particular psychic world of its author; it contains no wisdom, no spiritual grace. As for modern science, it neither possesses nor demands any beauty. Being purely analytic, it scarcely opens its eyes to a contemplative vision of things. When it studies man, for instance, it never contemplates his entire nature which is at once body, soul and spirit. If we make modern science responsible for modern technology, it is at the very basis of a whole world of ugliness. The least we can say is that modern science, in spite of all its learning and experience, is an unwise science. Perhaps the greatest lesson traditional Islamic art can teach us lies in the fact that beauty is a criterion of truth. If Islam were a false religion, if it were not a divine message but a system invented by man, could it have produced so many works of art endowed with everlasting beauty?

Here is the point where we must ask the question: 'What ought to be the rôle of the fine arts in Muslim education today?' The study of Islamic art, if undertaken with an open mind and without the European prejudices we have mentioned, is a way to approach the spiritual background of the whole of Islamic culture. The same is true for all traditional art. The main shortcoming one has to avoid is the academical mentality that considers all works of art from earlier centuries as purely historical 'phenomena' which belong to the past and have very little to do with our actual life. We cannot even understand art, it seems, without knowing the historical circumstances of its birth. Against this relativistic point of view we gladly affirm that for the Muslim, the great mosques of Kairawan, Cordova, Cairo, Damascus, Ispahan, Herat and so on belong as much to the present as to the past, insofar as it is still possible to realize the state of mind of those who created them. Nor does it make sense to say: 'We are living in another time and therefore cannot take those famous buildings as a model for contemporary mosque architecture.' Let us not run after time — it will always be faster than we are — but let us ask what is timeless in the art of our spiritual ancestors. If we recognize it, we shall also be able to make use of it within the inevitable framework of our own epoch.

Historical research is useful; it gives answer to questions like these: When has this mosque been built? Who built it? Who paid for its construction? What were its nearest models? and so on. But Muslim education in the fine arts should not stop there; it should point primarily to the actual values of Islamic art. Let the students know the technical proceedings of the various arts from pottery to the vaulting of a dome; let them discover the geometrical figures from which the proportions of a given building have been developed. To be brief, let them experience, in their minds at least, the very genesis of a work of art. For the great artistic legacy — whether it is lost or only neglected, whether it can be rediscovered or not — is traditional art itself, not as an object but as a method, joining a technical know-how to a spiritual vision of things, a vision which has its source in *tawhīd*.

Chapter Four
Education in the Traditional Arts and Crafts and the Cultural Heritage of Islam

Jean-Louis Michon (Ali Abd al-Khaliq)

Born 1924, French; since 1972 and at present Chief Technical Adviser in charge of a UNESCO-UNDP programme for the preservation of traditional arts and crafts and the establishment of the General Survey of Cultural Property in Morocco (State Ministry for Cultural Affairs); Lic. in Law, Dipl. Nat. School for Political Sciences; Ph.D. in Islamic Studies (Sorbonne); lic.ès-lettres (English lang.) Art school and Dipl. in Architectural draughtsmanship in Lausanne, Switzd; 3 years teaching (English language and literature) in Damascus, Syria; 5 years architectural work (restoration of historical monuments) in Switzerland—20 years work within the United Nations family of organisations (linguistic, editorial and conference services; programme of technical assistance). Many travels and study tours in most parts of the Islamic world and India, Japan, the USA; publications include: '*The Autobiography (Fahrasa) of a Moroccan Sufi: Ahmed Ibn 'Ajiba (1747–1809)*', translated from Arab mss. into French with introd. and notes — Leyde (Brill) 1969; '*The Moroccan Sufi Ahmad Ibn 'Ajiba and his Mi'raj, a glossary of the technical terms of Islamic mysticism*' (in French; Paris, Vrin, 1974); Various articles, papers and conferences on subjects related to the meaning and value of Islamic institutions, arts and crafts of Islam and their preservation.

Basic Considerations: Art is an Integral Component of the Islamic Way of Life

Man, who was created 'in the most beautiful stature' (Qurān 95, 4) and as 'the image of God' (*hadīth*) has received from the Divine Artisan, together with the gift of language, the faculty to express outwardly, by means of artistic forms, the realities and intuitions perceived by his inner senses. Islam, having been sent to remind all mankind that 'I created them only that they should adore Me' (Qurān 51, 57), has brought with it, together with the Divine Message and as a special favour embodied in the Revelation, ways and means to develop the artistic faculties among the believers and put them to use for the propagation of faith and for the strengthening of the virtuous life among the *ummah*.

That beauty, both in the world of nature as it was made by the Creator and in the works of those craftsmen whose hands are guided by authentic knowledge and vision (*'ilm al-yaqīn wa' ayn al-yaqīn*), may be an incentive to remembrance and worship of *Allāh ta 'ālā* is repeatedly taught by the Holy Qurān and *Hadīth*. All the *āyāt* of the Holy Book, which describe, with inimitable harmony of words and splendour of images, the beatitudes of perfect life in the Hereafter and the generous favours which the Lord has bestowed upon His creatures, are meant to arouse in the hearts of men a strong and sincere impulse to surrender themselves to the Unique Master of all perfection. Whereas such sayings as 'God is Beautiful and He Loves beauty' (*Allāhu Jamīlun yuḥibbu 'l-jamāl*) and 'Careful achievement belongs to piety' (*al-itqānu min al-taqwā*) are meant to encourage those who are endowed with an artistic gift to put it to the service of their faith.

It is because of these basic tenets and this constant appeal to the aesthetic sense in man that Muslims displayed from the start a remarkable ability to integrate various artistic techniques and forms already used in the different regions opened to Islam. And it was the originality and vigour of these tenets that, together with the specific prescriptions of the *Sharī'ah* including ritual practice (*'ibādāt*) and social behaviour (*mu'āmalāt*) gave rise to a new style of art, recognizable only as 'Islamic', an art which has been part and parcel of the Islamic way of life throughout time and space.

Islamic art responds to a number of fundamental needs of the community. 'Only that they should adore Me', as the Qurān states, means that human life is intended to be a perpetual act of devotion and remembrance of its Author. It implies, *inter alia*, that men should be surrounded in their day-to-day existence, and not only at the moments of prayer and ritual worship, with an ambience composed of persons, natural forms and man-made objects which help them to remember God constantly and pay Him their debt of gratitude. This is achieved in society through the adherence of all believers to the *Sharī'ah*, which creates a dense network of sacred behaviour, both individual and collective, among the *ummah*. It is also achieved, in the material frame of daily life, by the spiritual imprint this frame receives by means of artistic expression. It is precisely the function of artists and craftsmen to translate the ideals of Islam into an aesthetic language of forms and patterns that will be embodied in the architectural and ornamental features of the sanctuaries as well as in the humble utensils used in the household.

The Scope of Islamic Art: A Few Definitions

According to the Islamic perspective, which stresses the absolute supremacy of the rights of God over and above the rights of man, artistic creativity is nothing but a God-given predisposition (*isti'dād*) which has to be used as an aid to celebrate the greatness of *Allāh ta'ālā* and walk upon the Straight Path to Him. The artist, then, is just a servant of God like all other human beings and does not belong to an out-of-the-ordinary category of individuals. The rôle he has to play in the community, as said above, will be best achieved if he is able, by unselfish service and attentive concentration, to make himself a faithful interpreter of the Islamic Tradition. Whence the link that has always been observed between intense religious practice, high morals, social ethics and high artistic achievements, as for example among members of the handicraft guilds (*hantah, futuwwah*) of the classical, and even more recent, periods.

Another prominent feature which dominates all aspects of Islamic civilization and among them the field of artistic production is the unitarian, or integrative, approach which aims at imprinting all human affairs and activities with the seal of Divine Unity (*tawhīd*). The fundamental tendency precludes making a clear-cut distinction between the material and spiritual planes. In fact Islamic art has never known anything like the distinction made in the West in recent times between 'pure art' (also called 'fine arts' or 'art of art's sake') and 'applied art' (or 'utilitarian art'), the first type aiming at provoking a mere aesthetical satisfaction, and the second responding also to some useful purpose. The arts of Islam, as indeed all traditional arts, are always 'functional', that is, useful, whether their usefulness be directly of a spiritual order (like that of a *miḥrāb* decorated with an irradiation of entrelaces and Quranic verses) or whether they confer upon the objects used in everyday life a distinctly qualitative character.

It would be, therefore, artificial and misleading to differentiate between the artist and the craftsman, or 'art' and 'craftsmanship', two notions which are expressed in the Arabic language by one and the same word, *al-fann*. One can still observe today that most traditional craftsmen, even among such humble professions as those of the shoemaker, weaver or ironsmith, may be termed 'artists' in the sense that they possess a virtual, if not always actual, creative power and that they are able to shape and decorate their products with renewed forms and patterns which remain consistent with the style and spirit of the traditional milieu.

We will find, certainly, in the community, a number of crafts which by their nature, do not lend themselves to any artistic production. Such operations like tanning or dyeing leather skins or carding wool and spinning it into a thin thread before using it on the weaver's loom must not, however, be detached from the whole artistic process to which they belong and from the final result to which they contribute. Moreover, an artistic component of some kind, in the form of work songs, special costumes, corporative rituals and festivals, is frequently associated with professional practice and constitutes a valuable component of the traditional culture.

To sum up what has just been said, we must consider as pertaining to the traditional arts and crafts of Islam those activities which are characterized by the transmission from father to son, or from master to apprentice, of the rules, standards and processes that constitute 'craftsmanship'; a transmission which, however, does not entail mere imitation nor stagnation but warrants a conceptual and technological stability in which the traditional craftsmen of Islam have found, for centuries, inexhaustible possibilities of renewal and adaptation.

The Decadence of the Islamic Arts and Crafts: a Few Causes and Effects

It is a well-known fact that the traditional arts of Islam, which preserved a remarkable vigour up to modern times, have suffered considerable loss since about the beginning of the present century. Not only has the massive aggression of industrial products proved destructive to a number of handicrafts, but the legitimate desire felt by most under-developed countries to eliminate their economic backwardness has led them to modernize their own industries on purely 'Western' lines. In so doing, they have paid very little attention to such sectors as traditional arts and crafts which at first sight seemed difficult to integrate into a modern process of development.

Along with its economic and technological ideas, the West has exported to the East, including Islamic countries, its humanistic and materialistic concepts which, in many ways and fields, have caused subtle alterations in the East's traditional, that is, fundamentally God-oriented way of life. Thus the 'élitist' view of art, whereby artistic creation constitutes a special domain of activity, separated from the so-called 'ordinary life', has spread widely into the Islamic world from Europe where it has been prevalent since the end of the Middle Ages. Contrary to its own genius, much of the world of Islam has become accustomed to viewing art, including its own, as a marginal activity, a simple matter of taste and affinity left to the appreciation of each individual.

There was no reason then to regret the disappearance of many objects of current use that had received, for many centuries, the typically Islamic touch given to them by the traditional craftsmen, nor to resist their replacement by ugly products of modern industry. Neither was it considered that adoption of Western fashions whether in dress or in the style of house furnishing might have anything to do with the preservation of genuine Islamic values. The combined effect of this indifference and shift in taste has been to deprive the traditional craftsmen of their earlier clientèle, especially the well-to-do, a class which was the most sensitive and open to Western influences.

The impact of the modern concepts and forms of art has also had several consequences for the artists themselves. *Firstly*, it has caused the emergence of a new class of artists who, like their Western models, consider art as a means of self-expression and, therefore, place themselves outside the realm of tradition, that is, adherence to principles and rules belonging to a higher, supra-individual order of reality. *Secondly*, traditional craftsmen have had a growing tendency to borrow formal elements of Western origin which are frequently in patent contradiction with the spirit of Islamic art. The invasion of naturalistic representations on carpets and tapestries, and the baroque or 'modern style' designs adopted for many a piece of furniture — otherwise carefully carved or incrustated — are just a few examples of this kind of contamination.

In face of so many dangers and adverse factors, both from outside and inside, what attitude should be adopted? Should one accept the decadence, and final elimination of the traditional handicrafts of Islam as an unavoidable fact, a ransom which has to be paid for the acquisition of technological progress? We do not think so, and there are good and realistic grounds to believe that a renaissance of traditional arts and crafts is not only desirable but also possible and feasible.

Education in the Islamic Arts and Crafts: a Necessity

As the element of 'transmission' of both ethical rules and technical methods is a prerequisite for the very existence of traditional arts, there would be no point in attempting a vigorous revival of Islamic arts and crafts if continuity had already come to an end. Traditional arts and crafts, like the life of the communities to which they belong, do not accept interruption but require the careful initiation of the younger generation by the elders into their basic lore and practice.

Fortunately, a considerable reservoir of skilled artistic craftsmanship still exists in the Islamic world. All the great cities of Islam, from Isfahan to Fes, passing by Damascus, Istanbul, Cairo and Tunis, shelter bodies of craftsmen who retain the qualities of their ancestors: humble dedication to their work, perfect honesty, deep piety and, on the technical plane, sureness of aesthetic judgment, skillful hands, and ability to make the best use of a given material or substance according to its intrinsic nature. The same may be said of many smaller communities and rural areas, especially those which are relatively isolated and where the products of industry do not penetrate too rapidly. In such places one can still find a whole range of genuinely artistic activities which continue to be rooted in daily life and necessities but, being exposed to the threats of rapid change, are also worthy of the greatest attention.

Considering the range and severity of adverse factors that can impede a normal programme for traditional arts and crafts, policy measures must be devised and applied, mainly at the governmental or state level, to correct the imbalance created by the disruption of the old methods and the emergence of new systems of economic relationships. Some Eastern countries have shown a remarkable readiness and ability to tackle these problems. The extraordinary success met by Japanese or Indian handicraft products today, in both the national and foreign markets, is largely due to the protective policies displayed by these governments. It proves with glaring evidence that such efforts are a valuable investment and that a policy of preservation of the national arts is by no means incompatible with the highest degrees of technological development.

A policy aiming at safeguarding and promoting the cultural heritage, and especially its living component represented by traditional craftsmen, will necessarily include a number of measures: financial aids and subsidies, facilities for the purchasing of raw materials and the marketing of finished products, social security benefits and the like. Although such measures, which have already shown their effectiveness, should be shared and studied by all interested countries, they will have to be adapted to local circumstances and conditions.

In all cases, however, the educational aspect will play a leading role in a protective policy of this kind. This is true not only because transmission of the rules and techniques of the arts is the *conditio sine qua non* of their continued existence, but also because the fundamental reason why the arts and crafts of Islam have to be maintained is that they are outward expressions and convincing messengers of an ideal, spiritual conception of life. To assimilate this ideal and spirit, so that it will become a permanent and genuine source of inspiration, Muslim craftsman will need a type of education where religious teaching, personal and professional ethics, as well as technical training, are closely intertwined.

The Different Types and Levels of Education in Arts and Crafts

A. The Apprenticeship System

For centuries, an integrated approach to art teaching had been most adequately ensured by the apprenticeship system with its three successive degrees: apprentice, workman, master. It was linked, in the cities, with the existence of the craftsmen's guilds and, in the rural areas, with tribal and patriarchal modes of life. Due to many recent transformations, including the introduction of compulsory education, concentration of the means of production in large workshops, disruption of corporative structures and similar causes, the old system has been largely abandoned and, where still functioning, is usually confined to the poorest sections of traditional society.

Some corrective measures have been successfully applied to retain the benefits of the age-old apprenticeship system while avoiding its present-day handicaps. Placement of apprentices by governmental agencies in agreed workshops is the most common practice: the 'master' responsible for their education may be subsidized by the government, or himself pay a small stipend to the apprentice; the latter may attend an ordinary school at special hours, or receive a complementary general and technical education in a specialized institution (professional or craft school).

A collective form of apprenticeship is also adopted in several countries where children — generally those who have already completed a primary course of education, at the age of thirteen years as an average — are given two or three years of professional training in official workshops run by the government. Although this system may have obvious social advantages in situations where many young people cannot afford to pursue secondary studies and must be able to sustain themselves as rapidly and early as possible, it cannot be considered a satisfactory method for the preservation of high quality craftsmanship. The excessively short duration of the training period and the predominantly utilitarian orientation of the teaching are, however, open to possible improvements.

B. Schools of Traditional Arts and Crafts

Whatever the importance and usefulness of the apprenticeship system for the training of a sufficient number of skilled craftsmen in the many sectors of handicrafts might be, there is still room for a more refined and elaborate type of training specifically designed to ensure the preservation and transmission of highly qualitative arts and crafts. The aim of this training should go a long way beyond the theoretical and practical mastery of one art. It should include acquisition of a good level of general education, technical knowledge and information in the different branches of Islamic art. It should prepare an élite of craftsmen and teachers who could occupy key positions in apprenticeship centres, official or private institutions for research and promotion of handicrafts, museums and schools of traditional arts, and services in charge of restoration and rehabilitation projects for historical buildings and cities, handicraft cooperatives and the like.

A standard model for such a school will be proposed in the following sections. It is not a mere theoretical and abstract construction, but is based on an actual experience that is currently under way in one Islamic country, namely Morocco. However, it has been reduced here to its essential components so as to make it more generally applicable to a number of diverse situations as may be encountered in other Islamic regions.

A Standard School of Traditional Arts: Conditions of Admission and Duration of the Studies; the Curriculum

The school is open to children from the age of twelve who have obtained their certificate of primary studies or given proof that they have successfully completed these studies. Admission is subject to an entrance examination which includes tests in Arabic writing and visual aptitude.

The period of studies extends over seven years, distributed as follows:

(a) First year (orientation) allows access by the pupils to all the different workshops, which gives them a general initiation into artistic activities and facilitates the placement of each pupil in the branch corresponding best to his taste and ability.
(b) Three years of training in the chosen craft; after completion and passing the practical and general/theoretical examinations, a diploma of 'skilled craftsman' in the specific branch is granted (the pupil may then leave the school and establish himself as an independent craftsman if he so wishes).
(c) Three years of specialization in the already chosen craft, with practical training in the other crafts pertaining either to the same category of techniques (e.g., incrustations, which may be either in wood or metal; engraving and sculpture which may be in stone, wood or plaster), or to the same family of materials (e.g., pottery and tile mosaics; weaving of wool, silk and cotton; using different techniques on leather, wood, metal and the like).
(d) Completion of these final three years and passing the terminal examinations leading to the diploma of 'Master in Traditional Art.'

The curriculum is such that it should ensure, throughout the study period, an equal distribution between the general and theoretical training given in the classrooms and the practical training given in the workshops. If one takes as a norm a schedule of 40 hours per week, 20 hours would be occupied by classroom work and 20 by workshop teaching, respectively.

The general and theoretical subjects would include:

(a) The Arabic language
(b) A foreign language
(c) Religious and social education
(d) Mathematics (arithmetic, algebra, geometry)
(e) Accounting, with notions of commercial law and management techniques
(f) Natural sciences: physics, chemistry, material technology
(g) History: national, general, with special emphasis on the history of Islamic civilization and art
(h) Geography
(i) Physical education and sports
(j) Technical draughtsmanship

(k) Arabic calligraphy
(l) Geometry of regular figures.

Practical teaching would include, for example, the following subjects:

(a) Stone and brick: masonry, including stone carving and brick decoration.
(b) Metalwork
- copperwork
- wrought iron, including damascenery
- silver and goldsmith work, jewelry
- other crafts, like bronze melting
(c) Woodwork
- carpentry
- joinery, sculpture
- painting and illumination (also practised on other flat surfaces, including paper)
- marquetry and incrustations
(d) Stucco
(e) Ceramics
- pottery
- tile mosaics
(f) Glass
(g) Leatherwork
- bookbinding, including the different techniques of leather decoration
- saddlery
(h) Textiles
- carpet weaving
- other woven materials
- sewing and embroidery.

The stress laid, within the classroom teaching, on such matters as calligraphy and the polygonal (regular figures) geometry needs some clarification. 'Arabic calligraphy', as my respected friend Mr. Titus Burckhardt remarked in a joint paper we prepared for UNESCO some years ago, 'is, with its synthesis of rhythm and form, like a key to Islamic art and, at the same time, the touchstone for the mastership of a given style. Exercise of calligraphy in all its stylistic variations determines a certain mode of thinking and imagining that is recognizable in all branches of Islamic art'. As for the formative value of polygonal geometry, a discipline which the artists of Islam have brought to incomparable mastery, I leave also to a connoisseur, Mr. Keith Critchlow, the merits of having demonstrated the reasons for its efficacy: 'Islam's concentration on geometric patterns draws attention away from the representational world to one of pure forms, poised tensions and dynamic equilibrium, giving structural insight into the workings of the inner self and their reflection in the universe (*Islamic Patterns*, London, 1976).

The teaching of art history should be of a predominantly visual character, which means that it should not aim at presenting pupils with only dates and scientific terms, but at feeding their visual imagination. Without excluding the comparative method, whereby parallels may be traced with other art forms and styles, the teaching should concentrate on Islamic art with practical value for the pupils. It should help them, above all, to acquire a clear consciousness of what constitutes the unique nature and beauty of Islamic art. Also, by illustrating the richness of variations that have been evolved throughout time and space to express fundamental themes, it will stimulate a desire to reach that degree of perfection in craftsmanship where it becomes possible to have diversity without detracting from unity.

For the teaching of art history, use of some visual aids and iconographic documentation will be necessary. These should best be borrowed from a central bureau of documentation and research that would be created as a part of the school and which would include different kinds of archives: photographs, slides, drawings and, if possible, cassettes and cinema films. The bureau would also comprise a library and some exhibition rooms containing good examples of different arts and crafts including some made by the pupils themselves and illustrating a wide variety of ornamental patterns.

Wherever possible, the schools should be situated in the historical quarters of old cities. Such sites have manifold advantages: for the pupils themselves, who will generally live inside the city itself and will not find themselves transplanted out of their traditional ambiance; and for the historical quarters which will benefit from the presence of new centres of cultural activity. It is very likely that the visits paid by teachers and pupils to the neighbouring craftsmen and historical buildings, either on an individual basis or on the occasion of 'open-air classes', will bear fruitful results in the way of rehabilitating the ancient *medinas*.

Higher Education

The training of teachers, who should be at the same time good practitioners and reliable transmitters of different branches of Islamic art, does not answer all the conditions that are needed on the educational plane for a renaissance of the arts of Islam. Some categories of personnel, e.g., those who will be responsible for programmes and activities linked with the preservation and promotion of Islamic artistic heritage, have yet to be trained. They include museum curators, teachers in the history and technology of art, architects, restorers of historical buildings, archaeologists and cultural anthropologists (specialized in the folk arts and crafts of Islam).

Such specialists should receive their training, on the one hand, at the university — where chairs should be created for the teaching of Islamic art, archaeology and ethnology — and, on the other hand, in specialized institutions which might be grafted upon already existing ones or, otherwise, created anew. The present solution adopted by most Islamic countries, consisting of reliance upon centres of specialized training that exist abroad, should not be regarded as satisfactory. Not only do they not provide sufficient numbers of specialists for the cultural services of the Muslim nations (partly because of the all too-famous 'brain-drain' problem), but they give no guarantee that such training will be oriented towards solving specific problems linked with the national Islamic heritage.

A typical institute for the study and preservation of the Islamic cultural heritage would comprise the following sections: general survey and documentation (on historical and natural monuments and sites, museum and other collections, traditional and folk arts), training and research (with courses on such subjects as Islamic architecture and arts, field surveys in ethnology and anthropology and laboratory research for the preservation of cultural property), and publications, information and public relations.

Apart from its purely academic functions, such an institute would be used as a consultative body and as a coordinating organ between all the governmental authorities concerned with the preservation of cultural heritage. It could also take an active part in the planning and execution of rehabilitation programmes. Such institutes might be created either at the national level or, when indicated, at a regional level under agreement between several countries.

Education of the General Public

Since it is in the very nature and goal of Islamic art to penetrate and shape the whole framework of life, a programme of rehabilitation of traditional arts and crafts can only be meaningful and reach its desired purpose if it involves the conscious adhesion and willing participation of the whole community. However, from what has been said about the insidious influence of Western models on many sections of the population, it is obvious that a serious educational effort, amounting in some cases to a real 'reacculturation', will have to be undertaken so as to bring the value of the Islamic arts once again to the eyes and minds of Muslims themselves.

The arguments, as well as the ways and means to be used in this campaign, will to a large extent be the same as those generally recommended for the rehabilitation of Islamic values. Some specific suggestions can, however, be made on the subject of art education. Sensitivity to traditional art forms should start at an early age. Children are usually deeply influenced by the toys with which they play, and presenting them with a miniature handloom instead of a mechanical device may entail a real difference in their future interests. When attending school, they should be led to discover the artistic treasures kept in museums and those which are still being made by skilled craftsmen. Those visits, and the tours that could be organized to historical places and monuments, should complement teaching given in the classrooms on national history, history of art and, in the near future, on the protection of the environment.

The mass-media such as the press, radio, television and cinema should devote more effort to the presentation of the riches of Islamic traditional art. Advertising genuine handicraft products and publicity should be included in current cultural programmes. Since examples originating in the West are still given much weight, many examples should be given of the strenuous efforts that are made by all Western nations, from Eastern Europe to the U.S.A., to revive their old handicrafts, preserve and rehabilitate their ancient cities and even recreate, at great pain and expense, homogeneous nuclei of a rural or urban way of life that has been extinct for many generations. The reasons for such a longing for the past should also be stressed: the ugliness, turmoil and strains of the modern cities, the depressing nature of factory work, and the fatigue resulting from the multiplication of needs.

Other means of cultural action should also be used, such as public lectures and discussions, conferences, symposia, temporary exhibitions and demostrations of art techniques. Such national activities as the month of traditional handicrafts celebrated in December each year in Morocco, or the week of historical monuments in Afghanistan, have great impact on the whole country. Some international fairs and exhibitions lend themselves to the fruitful advertisement of the arts and crafts of

Islam. In the final analysis, however, the best advertisement remains the individual Muslim who, by his personal conviction and example makes himself an educator — 'one who exhorts to the good', as the Holy Qurān states — among the community; the teacher who, while wearing neat traditional clothes, demostrates the beauty of calligraphy; the architect who, having an order to build a villa proposes a traditional type of design which admits participation of traditional craftsmanship and decoration.

All these efforts and contributions might give unexpectedly quick and widespread results. The adoption of Western fashion and customs has been, to a large extent, the result of passive and uncaring attitudes. For a great number of Muslims, then, the mere realization that they have been blinded by an inferiority complex, or that they have succumbed to a secret desire to taste an unknown fruit — even though somewhat poisonous — may suffice to restore pride and confidence in their own cultural values, letting them see with new eyes the wisdom and beauty of the formal universe built by their virtuous ancestors, the *salaf al-ṣāliḥ*.

Chapter Five
On Art and Education

Kazi A. Kadir

Born 1934, Pakistani; Associate Professor, Department of Philosophy, University of Karachi, Pakistan (since 1967). Previously, taught at Dacca University (1962-64); Peshawar University (1964-67); Head, Dept. of Fine Arts, University of Peshawar (1965-67); President of Logic and Metaphysics Section, Pakistan Philosophical Congress (1969); Chairman, Dept. of Philosophy, University of Karachi (1974-77). Publications include: *Modern Introduction to Logic* (1965) *Psychology and Education* (1972, Co-author); *Education and Philosophy of Education* (1973); *Monographs on 20th century Philosophy* (1973); *Sartre and God* (1975). Publications in collaboration with others: *Our Knowledge of the External World* (1963); *Existentialism* (1965); *Phenomenology* (1966); *Philosophy of History* (1967); *Philosophy of Science* (1971). Editor *Iqbal Review* (1969-72); *Jadeed Science* (1960-62) and (1967-77).

An artist, whether he be a painter, an illustrator of books, a decorator, or a designer, contributes to his society's emotional and material welfare.* Folk artists, craftsmen, painters and bookbinders hold a position which is at par with that of economists, educationists, scientists and technicians of a society. Along with the development of science and technology in a society goes the development of the aesthetic and sensibility of its people. When one lags behind the other, there is liable to be cultural imbalance and disharmony. The result can be disastrous if people are led to believe that artistic creativity is alien to cultural life. I will however not go into this theological controversy.[1]

A person can study Islamic art without necessarily being involved in a theological or philosophical discussion about the possibility of Islamic art or art in Islam. I take it as a matter of fact that the people who claim to be Muslims have produced painters, potters, architects, calligraphers, illustrators and designers. I am concerned with these people and with what they have created in their long cultural history for there is something very distinctive about their artistic creations. The distinctive features of their art are both 'positive' and 'negative.' Let us first enumerate some of these characteristic features.

---

*Art, in this paper refers to visual and plastic art; music, dance and literature are not mentioned. The paper deals with (a) the salient features of Muslim art, the source of inspiration of this art and (b) the rôle that art is expected to play in Muslim education and society of the next century *hijra*.

1. On the 'negative' side, Islamic art avoids, what we call, the pagan practices, that is, idol making. Muslim artists have usually avoided making life-size, life-like sculptures in the round. Even in a cosmopolitan environment a Muslim sculptor who renders life-size human figures in three dimensions is a rarity.[2]

2. This takes us to the second point, that of perspective. The dislike for pagan idolatory was identified with three-dimensional figures and hence early Muslim artists kept the element of depth out of their paintings. There is deliberate avoidance of perspective to remind the artist and the patron that a painting is a flat surface and that it should be kept like that. However, because of a more sophisticated attitude towards religious injunctions, in the Mughal Style of painting a sort of idealized perspective was introduced.[3]

3. If art in Islam has avoided pagan elements, it has also avoided depicting what are usually called the 'religious truths.' For example, when we refer to 'Christian art,' we mean the art in which Christian myths and symbols are depicted. This kind of religious element is missing in Islamic art and we do not talk of 'religious paintings' in Islam, in this sense. There is no authentic portrait of the Prophet and none of his companions nor of his wives. Moreover, there has never been a tradition, the way we have in Christian art, to paint the life of the Blessed Prophet.[4]

4. This brings us to the fourth and the 'positive' feature of Islamic art. This art does not revolve around individuals; it has a social orientation and is anchored in the common needs of men. An artist in Islam is a maker of useful things. He is a potter or a carpet and textile designer; he illuminates books, makes and decorates scientific instruments. His artistic genius finds expression in all branches of life.[5]

5. The Muslim artist shows a special concern for nature. For him nature is not alien, not something to be despised or eliminated from his spiritual and cultural life. This is an attitude which the artist in Islam shares with the Sufis, the poets and most of the philosophers in the Muslim world. What distinguishes the artist from a Sufi or a poet is the possession of tools he has at his disposal to convey this affinity between man and nature.[6]

6. Art in Islam is essentially calligraphic. One may legitimately ask why it is so. There are traditions and documents to tell us that (a) the Blessed Prophet was very particular about the written word and he personally supervised writing classes in Madina,[7] (b) trained scribes were needed to make the copies of the Holy Qurān so that the message of Allah could be sent to Muslim communities living in distant lands, (c) thirdly, the Holy Qurān directed the people to put in writing their commercial

and business dealings and not to leave their affairs to the vagaries of human memory.[8] Writing thus became important in Islam not only for religious purposes but for commercial reasons as well.

Calligraphy

We must, however, remember that writing is not calligraphy. In calligraphy we go beyond the purely functional to the aesthetic value of writing. Again, there is a tradition that the Blessed Prophet more than once pointed out the rules to distinguish one letter from another.[9] He thus emphasized the purely formal characteristics of various letters. Paying attention to the form of letters, I believe, is the genesis of calligraphy. Here we become interested not in *what a piece of writing says* but *how it looks*. This is to consider writing as a form of art. But to see all visual art-forms calligraphically is to develop different aesthetics. We will see how Islamic art grew out of these aesthetics. No doubt there have been exceptions to this principle but such exceptions are found in most human enterprises. No functional rule is free from them.

Calligraphy and Botanical Motifs

The formal differences of '*sīn*' and '*shīn*' to which the Blessed Prophet referred, soon inspired calligraphers to work out the decorative qualities of these Arabic letters. We find that both in manuscript as well as in lapidary writing the calligraphers evolved almost a dozen different shapes of *sīn*. '*Alif*', which is the first letter not only of Arabic, Persian and Urdu but also of the Divine Name *Allāh*, underwent a similar artistic transformation. The same was the case with '*bā*,' '*jīm*,' '*dāl*,' '*wāw*,' etc.[10] The words *Allāh, Lā, Rahmān* and *Rahīm* underwent an infinite variety of shapes.[11] But this variety exhibited common elements too and there was the presence of idealized botanical elements in various letter forms, for example, the date leaf, the date tree, the leaves of certain vegetables, and fruits which the Blessed Prophet was known to have liked such as olives, pomegranates, grapes, gourds and pumpkins.[12]

Calligraphy and the Human Form

Once it was realized that letter-forms can conveniently accommodate bold botanical motifs, the possibility of employing intricate floral motifs was also seen. We find various expert calligraphers such as al-Aḥwāl, al-Maharrī (786–833 A. D.) Ibn Muqlaʻ (886–940 A. D.), Ibn Durustī (872–958 A. D.) and Mīr ʻAlī Tabrīzī (1446 A. D.) prescribing rules for their art and linking written letters with objects of nature. Thus 'alif' should resemble an ear of barley, and the top of 'ṣād' should be like an apple pip. Calligraphers are reported to have been told in their dreams to look at the eye, the beak and the neck of the swan to see how round, convex and concave they were and to make these shapes the model of their calligraphy.[13] The artist or the calligrapher arrived at the position where he could see complete identity between the pictorial and the ideographic. The language sign not only conveys an idea, but it also has built-in sensory, visual natural forms. The 'alif' does not only look like an ear of 'barley', it resembles the human form too.[14] In the same way that an ear of barley swings high in the air, 'insān' (the human), the first-letter of which is 'alif', is not tied down to the gravitational pull of the earth. He is light like the forms of the swan; he moves like the tendrils of a grape vine. In this world there are curves and no straight lines.[15]

To study this dynamic quality we should turn to miniature painting. Miniature painting in Muslim art is a clue to the general attitude of the artist and society towards life. For them nature is not alien. The same attitude is found in classical Muslim architecture, whether residential, palatial or devotional.[16] Decorative motifs exploited by Muslim architects are both vegetal and calligraphic. Letters in the hands of the artist become moving tendrils and leaves. However, the desire to bring nature into the four walls of the house went beyond this decorative ingenuity. Classical Muslim architecture also, whether Indo-Pakistani, Iranian or Spanish, shows the same concern for nature.[17] Appreciation of the beauty of the written word and the love for nature have all along remained the essential elements of art in Muslim society.

It is this character of art which we ought to keep before us, not only because it is a part of our cultural heritage but because of its implications for the future. The future to which I allude is not far away. The industrial countries are already getting a glimpse of it. The reduction of working hours from 48 to 30 per week has increased leisure hours three-fold. To this may be added the time which the workers save or may be saving in travelling to and from the work area by very fast transport systems. Considering the present trend in city planning, the time spent in travelling to the office or factory may be eliminated altogether.[18] Making allowance for time spent per week by a city worker in sleeping, being with his family, work in the office or the factory and the like, he will have at least forty hours per week, six hours per day, with 'nothing to do.'[19] Muslim society has yet to face this 'leisure crisis' but one can foresee the coming state of affairs.

Economic plans, land reforms and educational policies in Pakistan, to take just one example, lead us to expect a fairly affluent population by the mid-eighties in that country. Both at the urban and the rural level more 'free time' than is available now is envisaged. In fact even today our rural population comprising farmers, peasants, and fruit growers have around a three months 'lay off' period per year. This is due mostly to their cropping and harvesting practices.[20] But by the introduction of mechanical methods the agricultural worker will have still more time free from work.[21] The farmer will spend this time, as he does to-day, in two kinds of activities: (i) family-centred, which has to do with such activities as repairing or constructing the house and arranging marriages of children or other members of the family; (ii) 'community-centred,' i.e. the sort of activities which are carried on and enjoyed in the presence of the other members of the community, for example, playing games, smoking and watching the T.V. at the community centre. We do not have widespread drinking in Muslim communities at the rural or even at the urban level.[22]

It is these 'community-centred' activities which are a 'cultural waste.' They lead to lethargy and create a sort of spiritual vacuum. This vacuum can be filled, apart from training in social ethics, by artistic activity. The machine has taken so much away from man, and whatever remains will be lost to lethargy and inactivity, unless of course man is reminded of the joy of using his skillful hands.

Artistic activities can be carried out if people know how to do so. One way to achieve this is to establish craft-villages (*madīnat al-fann*; *honarnagār*) where the techniques of the city and the talents of the town can meet.[23] Craft-villages are a complex of cottages of a dozen or so artists and craftsmen with their respective shops, kilns and the like. They also have research rooms, small modest museums and exhibition halls. These craft-villages should be located in easily accessible villages, not in the heart of big cities. It is believed that such craft-villages will provide opportunities for the rural dweller to learn to utilise his leisure in gainful, creative activities. They will also create a sense of 'belongingness' for the villager and fill the intellectual and emotional gap between the rural and the urban populations, the city and the town. Both communities will share the joint social and artistic venture of creating and appreciating beauty.

Art education, however, is not to be imparted merely to meet the impending 'leisure crisis.' It has still one more significant role to play in the Muslim community. We have already seen that art in Islam shows a special concern for nature. We have to revive this concern in our masses. The industrial nations, as shown above, are facing the 'leisure crisis' which Muslim communities have yet to encounter. However, both of us, the industrially advanced countries and the Muslim nations are confronted with the 'ecological crisis.' No doubt developing industries in Muslim countries have yet to reach the point where they become a hazard to human life.[24] We have yet to face the problem of industrial and chemical waste as the danger to our biotic system that it has become in industrial countries.[25] But the present apathy to nature, in the widest sense of the word, is a state of mind which ought to be looked into. Environmental experts are no longer satisfied with their strategy of fighting this crisis with merely 'scientific tools.' Need is felt to meet this challenge on an interdisciplinary level using talents from the social sciences as well as the humanities.[26] Environmental experts have already begun to talk about 'environmental aesthetics' and the need is felt to educate people in this direction. I believe that art education and artistic training can go a long way in making the present and future generations alive to environmental issues. It has been observed that mere training in environmental science does not make a person fight the 'ecological war' wholeheartedly. What is needed is love and concern for the beauty of the natural world.

Environmental aesthetics, as I understand the term, is concerned with the preservation, beautification and appreciation of the natural environment. A properly designed educational policy and an imaginatively framed syllabus for art education can generate a proper feeling for environmental beauty. Such an educational scheme, which needs to be spelled out by experts, would, I believe, revive our traditional concern for nature. We have heard so much about preserving natural beauty and wild life for tourist business or to earn foreign exchange.[27] It is high time that we thought of the spiritual significance of God's creation.

NOTES AND REFERENCES

1. *Ṣaḥīh Muslim*, vol. II, Delhi, 1937, sayings 2035-2039; K. A. C. Creswell: 'The Lawfulness of Painting in Early Islam,' *Islamic Culture*, vol. XXIV, 3, 1950, pp. 218-225. Creswell provides an impressive bibliography but incorrectly believes (p. 219) that there is no mention of painting in the Holy Qurān; K. Boulata: 'Classical Arab Art and Modern European Painting: A Study in Affinities,' *Muslim World*, Vol. LXIII, I, 1973, pp. 1-14. Boulata, however, misquotes the Holy Quran; see *ibid*., p. 9. See Shah Walīallāh, *Fiqh-i 'Umar*, Lahore, 1952, p. 320f.

2. This does not mean that human or animal motifs were not exploited by early Muslim artists or craftsmen. See in this regard the paintings in Qaṣr al-hayr (c728/A.H.) and Quṣayr 'Amra (c724-43/A.H.) of Umayyad Syria, also animal and 'mythical' figures carved on stone in the Seljuq period.

3. From Emperor Akbar's time (1542-1605 A.D.) and onwards. In some early Turkish miniature/book illustrations the concern for 'Volume' can be detected, for example the *Manāfi' al-hayawān* illustrated in 1294/A. H. at Maraghah. The figures of the two bears may be cited in this regard.

4. The exceptions in this regard are (i) *Mi'rāj-nāmah* (Herat 1436 Bibliothèque Nationale, Paris), (ii) A 16th c. Mughal miniature depicting a scene derived from the story of Noah's ark (Freer Gallery of Art, Washington/Smithsonian Institute), (iii) 'Madona and Child' paintings of Akbar-Jahāngīr's time. Also, (a) Johnson Album XIV (Folio Z, India Office Library).

5. H. Read, *The Meaning of Art*, London, 1963, p. 83; E. Kühnel, *Islamic Art*, London, 1963, and Kühnel, *Islamic Art and Architecture*, London, 1966, pp. 146, 164.

6. S. H. Nasr, *The Encounter of Man and Nature*, London, 1968, pp. 94-95, 97, 119; Nasr, *Islamic Studies*, Beirut, 1966, Chapter V, XIII; Boulata, 'The script itself takes the shape of an ostrich, an eagle, a peacock or other creatures . . . . It was as if they instinctively knew that praise of God is not performed with words alone but through His own creation . . .' *op. cit*., p. 10; and A. K. Jerazbhai, 'The Spirit of Islamic Art,' *Mahe Nau*, 1957, pp. 98-100.

7. M. Hamidullah, *Ahd-e-Navi Mein Nizami Hukumat*, Hyderabad, 1948, pp. 219-221.

8. Holy Qurān, II:282; also II:176.

9. Hamidullah *op. cit*., p. 291; Muhammad Fadallāh al-Anṣārī wa'l-Fārūqī (1102 A. H.), *Asrār al-khaṭṭ* quotes forty sayings of the Blessed Prophet about the virtues of calligraphy. See V. K. Bukhari, 'A Rare Manuscript on Calligraphy, *Islamic Culture*, vol. XXXVII, 2, pp. 92-99. I do not question or confirm the authenticity of these quotations but wish to point out the general attitude of the artist and the calligrapher towards his vocation, that it is somehow divinely or spiritually ordained as expressed by the words of the Blessed Prophet. See also, Abū Ḥayyān al-Tawḥīdī, *'Ilm al-kitābah*, trans. M. A. Chughtai, *Iqbal Review*, vol. VII, 4, 1967, pp. 74-100.

10. A. Arif. *Arabic Lapidary Kufic in Africa* (London, 1967), pp. 11-17, 33.

11. *Op. cit*., pp. 13.

12. *Ṣaḥīḥ Muslim* (Delhi, 1937), Vol. II, 1982-1986.

13. On Mīr 'Alī Tabrīzī see Ziauddin, *Moslem Calligraphy*; Shantinikitan, 1936, p. 65.

14. Jerazbhai *op. cit*., p. 99.

15. *Ibid*.

16. Claude Betley, *The Design and Development of Indian Architecture*, London, 1965, plates 3, 48.

17. A. U. Pope, *Persian Architecture*, London, 1965, plates 243, colum plates XXII, XXI, XVIII; C. M. Villers-Stuart, *Spanish Gardens*, London, 1929, pp. 4, 5, 17-18. Villers-Stuart maintains that the love of flowers and plants in the garden finally 'became

the paramount influence through Muslim art,' p. 4; E. Kühnel, *Islamic Art*, trans., Watson, London, 1966, pp. 146, 155, 164, 166, 167.

18. G. Holmes Perkin. 'The Regional City' in Woodburry (ed.), *Future of Cities in Urban Redevelopment*, Chicago, 1950, pp. 36–37; also William L. Salyton and R. Dewey in Woodburry, *op. cit.*, pp. 335–345.

19. Stanely Parker, *The Future of Work and Leisure*, London, 1971, p. 82.

20. D. N. McVean and V. C. Robertson, 'An Ecological Survey of Land Use and Soil Erosion in the West Pakistan and Azad Kashmir Catchment of the River Jhelum,' *Journal of Applied Ecology*, vol. VI, 1969, pp. 77–109.

21. Usmanullah, 'Agro-Chemical Industry and our Economy,' *Jadeed Science*, vol. XIV, 4–5, 1975, p. 49–59.

22. According to Parker, 'Leisure may be seen as a factor of cultural progress or cultural decline, for social integration or alienation; it may stimulate the involvement of the individual or lead him to irresponsibility towards himself or his kind. We must decide which of these alternatives are preferable,' *op. cit.*, p. 141.

23. Kazi, A. Kadir, 'Promotion of Visual Arts in Pakistan,' paper read at the Seminar on Visual Arts, Arts Council of Pakistan, Dec. 1974; also *Dawn* (Karachi), March 22nd, 1976.

24. Iqtidar H. Zaidi, 'Land Use Hazards in an Arid Environment: The Case of the Lower Indus Region,' in *Ecological Guidelines for the Use of Natural Resources in the Middle East and South West Asia*, IUCN, No. 34, 1975, pp. 38–60.

25. V. Nelson-Smith, 'The Effects of Oil Pollution and Emulsifier Cleansing upon Shore Life in South-West Britain,' *Journal of Applied Ecology*, vol. V, 1968, pp. 97–107; E. B. Cowell, 'The Effects of Oil Pollution on Salt-Marsh Communities in Pembrokeshire and Cornwall,' *Journal of Applied Ecology*, vol. VI, 1969, pp. 133–142.

26. *Ecological Guide Lines*, *op. cit.* See Resolutions No: 4 and 5 on environmental education and interdisciplinary studies.

27. S. H. Nasr, *Encounter of Man and Nature*, pp. 135–6.

Chapter Six
Translation: Problems and Methods

Peter Hobson (Ismā'īl 'Abdu'l-Bāqī)

Born Horsforth, U.K., 1924. B.A. (Hons) Founder Director and Research Director of the Islamic Environment Research Centre Ltd. Formerly, 1952–1969, Member of H.M. Foreign Office with extensive service in Japan, Far East and South East Asia. 1975–1976, Consultant on Islamic literature to the World of Islam Festival. Has wide experience in translation from Chinese, Japanese, Arabic, Indonesian, Sanskrit and various European languages.

Introduction

To translate is one thing; to speak about the art of translation — for at its best it is an art — is another. But, with God's help, I shall attempt to outline certain considerations and suggest certain principles on this subject. However, since the material of our craft is language, I must begin by briefly examining the nature of speech, of words, of language itself.

The Nature of Language

Language is a compassionate gift of God to Man in his fallen state: 'Then from his Lord was Adam accorded words, for his Lord turned back to him; verily He, even He, is the Ever-Returning, the all-Compassionate' (II; 37).

Now Man in his fallen state — or, in other words, after Adam's expulsion from the Garden — remains God's Vicegerent upon the earth, (*khalīfatu'llāh*) and has been granted not only the distinctive gift of human speech but also the gift of Revelation through the medium of Divine Speech: 'Then We said, "Get ye down all from here and whenever, as is sure, there shall come to you Guidance from Me, whoever follow My Guidance, on them shall be no fear neither shall they grieve"' (II; 38).

Here, then, in two contiguous verses of the Qur'ān, we have reference to the two primal poles of language: the Divine Speech of Revelation which, in the guise of human language, is a reverberation of the Absolute in the relative for the salvation of Man; and human language which is itself relative and imperfect, like all things in manifested creation — for only God is perfect — but which is a unique gift of God to Man whereby Man is distinguished and raised above all other animate beings. The supreme function of human language is prayer; thus language is a token of Man's innate nobility.

I have said '*innate* nobility', and here I am thinking of Man's primordial nature (*fiṭrah*), from which he can never be entirely severed without ceasing to be Man, but I am thinking also of the degeneracy of Man in this present age, and of the degeneracy of human language which devolves from this.

In Man's primordial state and situation, the speech with which Adam conversed with God and was taught all the Names and told them to the Angels, was clearly not dependent upon the bodily organs of speech and the vibrations of air, but was a direct operation of the Intellect (*al-ʿaql*), or the Spirit (*al-rūḥ*), echoing the Divine Speech of God symbolized by the Creative Word 'be!' (*kūn*) whereby to name a thing with its true Name was to seize upon it directly as it exists in Reality; in such a state, the Name was the Named and the vibration — or one might say radiation — was not in the air but, speaking metaphysically, in the ether. In this state, Adam's Speech and Knowledge surpassed that of the very Angels.

When, after the fall, Man entered into the bodily state, his language, having become terrestrial and dependent upon the bodily organs of speech and the vibration of the air, must nevertheless have long retained a celestial quality of purity and unity, for Mankind was created from a single soul.

Then, in the Revelations of Monotheism we find, referring to a far, subsequent date in the history of Mankind, the story of the Tower of Babel; the scattering of mankind and the dispersion of tongues. From this point we can perceive the division of mankind into ethnic groupings, each with a language appropriate to its circumstances, environment, psychology and form of worship — a continuous process of elaboration, and thereby of fragmentation, in which modes of thought brought about forms of speech, and speech determined, and limited, modes of thought. The constant dispersal and elaboration of human language away from its pristine unity and purity, together with the perceptible phenomena of phonetic decay, the loss of certain languages entirely and the impoverishment of meaning that overtakes words when they are constantly used in mundane contexts, is like a moving away from the Divine Centre or from the Divine prototype of Speech — from that True Speech which is ultimately symbolized for us in the Creative Word '*kūn*' and in the Speech which lies behind the outward language of Divine Revelation.

The present situation of the languages of mankind can be perceived by considering their divisions into the great language families — the Semitic, the Aryan, the Hamitic, the Bantu, the Sinic, the Turkic and so forth — each with their countless ramifications into sub-families, separate languages and dialects, literary modes and vernaculars and each containing the constant human and psychological categories of verbs, nouns, adjectives and so forth, and each with strengths and weaknesses. All of this must be understood in the light of a progressive exteriorization, or descent, of speech from the Intellect or from its seat in the Heart to the mind, to the brain and the vocal organs; from unity to multifariousness; from singleness and purity to multiplicity and relative decline; from the noble language of Revelation to everyday speech; from the direct perception of the Intellect to speculative reason (note in this context, the connection between 'logos and logic' and between '*nuṭq*' and '*manṭiq*'); from the abiding to the temporal (note the relative emphasis in modern languages on the precise definition of verbal tenses as compared with older tongues); from qualitative to quantitative considerations (it is instructive to note for example, that in certain Far Eastern languages, in which all nouns were formerly treated as collectives, it is now becoming habitual to use distinctive forms for singular and plural, and it is interesting to note how, in certain modern languages, certain verbs meaning 'to tell, relate, speak' are derived from verbs meaning originally 'to enumerate', e.g., 'to tell' or 'to recount' in English, '*raconter*' in French, '*bilang*' in modern, colloquial Malay, and so forth); from psychological subtlety to empiric matter-of-factness (note the total loss, or decay, in many, modern languages of such verbal modes as the optative, jussive, subjunctive or the passive voice as in colloquial Arabic — or the middle and the passive voices even in Greek and post-Vedic Sanskrit).

Finally, in this connection, I should mention that in none of the present languages of mankind do the root-forms of words survive as such; they are perceptible only as the forms from which other words are derived. Thus it is in theory possible to derive the vast majority of words in Sanskrit from 800 verbal roots, none of which are any longer used as such, but manifest their presence only in the words derived from them. Similarly, in Arabic, the triconsonantal roots shine through the words derived from them — as the noble words '*RAḤIMAH, RAḤMĀN, RAḤĪM, RAḤMAH, MARḤAMAH, RĀḤIM, ARḤAM* or *ARḤĀM* all glow with the root

$R = \underset{.}{H} = M$ — but the root itself is conceivable only as a kind of abstraction, like the glow of the sunset when the sun has sunk over the horizon, and this is so even though Arabic is the noblest and most primordial of surviving languages, a miracle preserved by God for His Last Revelation, surpassing in its phonology and morphology the most historically ancient forms of Semitic speech of which we have any record, the Code of Hammurabbi for example. 'Verily in this is a Sign for them that know' (XXX; 22).

And is it not perhaps significant that the word '*lughah*' should have come to be the habitual word in modern Arabic for 'language'? It does not appear in the Holy Quran at all — in the Holy Qurān the word '*lisān*' is used — and it is derived from the root $L-GH-W$ which has pejorative and worldly overtones as for example, in the Holy Quran: 'No vain talking (*laghwan*) will they hear therein nor incitement to sin, but only the utterance "Peace, Peace" '. (LVI; 25).

Almighty God said of Himself, speaking to men: 'and it is He that hath made you vicegerents of the earth, and hath raised some of you above others in rank that He may test you in what He hath given you' (VI; 165). Now this must apply to men in all their aspects and, in particular, to that aspect which distinguishes them from all other beings, namely, their speech. This means that all human speech, all the languages of men, are, in virtuality, such as to befit God's vicegerent on earth since all derive ultimately from God's gift to Adam; but as some men are higher than others in rank, so are certain tongues intrinsically more noble than others and, within single languages, certain forms — generally speaking those which are antecedent in time — are more noble than other forms. Thus, as is self-evident to Muslims, Arabic is 'higher in rank' than English, and classical Arabic is nobler than modern, colloquial Arabic; but perhaps it is less self-evident that such gradations exist as between members of quite other language families or within, say, modern European languages and that, for example, the English of the 17th century is intrinsically more noble than that of the present day.

In insisting, in these opening remarks, upon the decline of language, particularly, and in accelerating fashion, in our own day, and in dwelling upon certain of the, metaphysically speaking, necessary reasons for this decline, I may well appear to be digressing into considerations that are highly abstract and hardly relevant to the problems we are discussing. However, I do so for two reasons: firstly, because I do not believe that any translator concerned with serious translation, particularly of the word of God or of God's Saints, or really of any religious subject, can consider himself qualified for his task unless he take account of these facts; and secondly, because their consideration effectively destroys two modern Western notions which are broadly accepted, willingly or only half-consciously, by most people in our age, namely — in the context of linguistics as in other fields — the notions of equality and progress.

More precisely, these are the notions that, firstly, any one language can be transposed into any other by a purely technical and almost mechanical process and that, when the resources of one language appear to be inadequate, it is simply a question of devising new words or of borrowing them from other tongues; and secondly that modern languages with their vast panoply of new words for new ideas, their 'scientific' precision and their rhetorical richness are somehow superior to older tongues, and that traditional ideas as expressed in the older languages are either best discarded in whole or in part, or are well served by being restated in a modern idiom, which is not necessarily true, and certainly not in the majority of cases. Both notions are fundamentally false.

The Problems of Translation

The above considerations and caveats should not be taken to mean that translation is in principle inadvisable, or that men are not entitled sometimes to be addressed in the language of their country and time to which, after all, their minds are, in the first place, attuned by earthly circumstance. However, bearing them in mind as cautionary and limiting observations, let us now turn to the more concrete problems of serious translation.

The first problem is the following: to translate means in effect to reshape, or even to recreate, an original text in another language; in this process part of the original — including its sound — is inevitably lost and something new — something which was not in the original — is added in compensation; the problem is to determine what may justifiably be lost and what added.

The translator's solution to this problem must clearly depend on the intrinsic nature of the text — whether, for example, it is a Sacred Text or otherwise — on the nature and 'rank' of the original language and on the expressive potentialities and standing of the language into which he is translating. There are even cases when one would conclude that translation should not be attempted at all.

The extreme case — it would be better to say the supreme case — concerns the translation of the texts of Divine Revelation from the language chosen for them by Almighty God into the modern idiom of any language; strictly speaking, such translation is frankly impossible, for what is lost in the process is irreplaceable and what is added is presumptious to a greater degree or less. In the first place, there is the element in Divine Speech that is supra-rational or, if you will supernatural — a reverberation of glorious sound and, indeed, of what lies beyond sound in a dimension not accessible to human reason but apprehended, with various degrees of profundity depending upon the reader or listener, by the heart and soul and yet, being supra-personal, transcending them. In the second place there are innumerable layers of meaning and possible interpretation — macrocosmic, microcosmic, mythological, allegorical, symbolical and so forth — even at the outward meaning of words and in the reverberation of verbal roots, and all these pose intractable problems of selection.

I am thinking chiefly, of course, of the Holy Qurān and also of the *Aḥādīth qudsiyyah*, but similar considerations have applied to the translation of the Bible from Hebrew and Greek — there being no single sacred language in Christianity covering both Revelation and worship — into the various languages of the Christians. To mention this here may seem irrelevant, but there are lessons in it for Muslims: the Bible is immeasurably reduced — and actually traduced and betrayed — when it is translated into, for example, modern English of any category, literary or colloquial; however in the noble translation of the 17th century known as the King James Version, made when the English language was at its peak and when it had not yet been corrupted by all the trivial uses to which it has been put more recently, the Bible retains the unmistakable stamp of its Divine Origin, and it has immeasurably enriched the English language. Nevertheless one should take note of, and ponder, the fact that the movement effectively to replace the Latin Bible by translations into the various ethnic languages of Christianity did, in fact, coincide with the decline of Christianity.

However, to return to the Holy Qurān, in principle it is untranslatable. If, however, to meet the abnormal exigencies of our times, it be considered necessary to attempt to render its outward meaning into tongues other than the original Arabic, then the task must be approached with fear and trembling. Only languages of great cultural standing should be entertained and, of these, the most noble forms; for it is not permissible to translate God's Word into mean and colloquial vernaculars. The translators must be pious Muslims; the purpose of any new translation should be, in the case of an attempted rendering into a non-Islamic language, or if the translation is mainly intended for non-

Muslims, to help to draw people to Islam and, in the case of using a fresh Islamic language, or if the translation is intended mainly for Muslims, to draw the readers to the Arabic original. The Arabic original should in principal always accompany the translation; and it should always be clearly understood, and stated, that no translation can possibly replace, or be any kind of substitute for, the original. These points are so self-evident that I apologize for making them; but it is not certain that they will necessarily be quite so self-evident to future generations.

To turn now to less weighty applications of what I termed the first problem of translation — namely, to what extent it is permitted to a translator, in reshaping his material, to discard certain elements and to add others in compensation — the solution of the problem must depend upon the relationship between the languages concerned. If these are the languages of peoples who share a common cultural heritage and hence a common psychological pattern that is reflected in their modes of thought and if, as a result, their languages have a great deal of vocabulary in common derived from a single source, then, provided the translator is competent, the technical problems are very few; it becomes largely a matter of transposition of idiom in which very little actual reshaping is involved. The same is largely true if the languages involved are cognate or, at least, members of a single linguistic family; but, by and large, cultural and religious affinity is a closer bond than linguistic affinity. It is, for example, a simpler matter to translate between Persian and Turkish, which belong to quite separate language families, than it would be between Arabic and Maltese, which belong to the same Semitic stock, especially if the subject were a religious one, for in the latter case one would need to bridge the cultural and religious divide.

The simplest categories of translation are therefore those in which there is a coincidence of cultural background, language family and historical period, that is — to take the most straightforward instances — as between all the modern languages of Europe such as, for example, modern French, Spanish, Italian and Portuguese or, again, between modern German, Dutch and any Scandinavian language. The next category, in order of simplicity, is when there is a coincidence between general cultural background and historical period although different language families are involved, such as between modern English and Hungarian, for example, or as between classical Arabic and classical Persian or classical Malay. The next category is when there is a certain coincidence of cultural background but not of language family or historical period, as between classical Arabic and, let us say, modern Bengali or modern Indonesian. It is, in fact, generally better in these cases to translate from one classical tongue into another classical idiom. The category of greatest difficulty is encountered when the translator has, as it were, no coincidences or affinities to lean upon but is required to cross cultural and religious divides, linguistic boundaries and time barriers; such are the difficulties encountered if, to take an extreme case, one were translating from classical Arabic into modern Chinese or even, in fact, into modern English, which is often entered upon far too lightly.

It appears to me to follow from this somewhat abstract analysis that, in order to lighten the translator's task, one should build upon the efforts of others: if a successful translation involving the crossing of, for example, one, two or all three of the barriers I have mentioned is once achieved, then it should serve as a pediment for other translations into further tongues, for there is really no point in crossing the same bridge twice. In other words if, for example, a successful rendering is made into French of a difficult text of classical Arabic, it is probably far more sensible and practical to translate the French directly into English, or German or into any other modern European language required, than to translate afresh from the original Arabic.

We must now turn to the second great problem of translation, the more technical one, which might be described as the lexicographical problem; it is, of course, inseparable from the first and it is partly in consideration of the lexicographical factor that I have ventured the recommendation at the end of the preceding paragraph. In brief, there exist excellent and comprehensive dictionaries, general and specialized, between all the main European languages, and there are sound historical reasons for this; but such is not the case as between all the various ethnic languages of Islam, or even between, on the one hand, the principal literary languages of Islam — let us say Arabic, Persian, Turkish, and Urdu for example — and the various languages of Europe, on the other. Moreover, such dictionaries as exist — and indeed such grammar books as exist — are of varying quality. As between English, or French, and Arabic there are excellent dictionaries; as between Bengali and Dutch, for example, I should very much doubt if this were so, and I should be surprised if there were adequate dictionaries between Arabic and Chinese despite the fact that there is an Islamic community of several tens of millions in China. And again, even in those cases where very good general dictionaries exist, it is far from certain that they are adequate in the specialized area of the religious vocabulary which more particularly concerns this gathering.

A further aspect of this problem is that of the standardization of terminology in order to ensure that one and the same term should not be rendered by quite different equivalents at the hand of different translators. For example, should '*rasūl*' be translated into English as 'Apostle', 'Envoy', 'Messenger' or 'Prophet', or are all acceptable, depending on the context or on the personal preference of the translator? Or, again, should the original term, if it be of frequent occurrence, simply be incorporated in transcription into the new language? This is, of course, the traditional solution to this problem adopted by languages sharing the same spiritual inspiration and heritage; thus, all the languages of Islam contain a large element of key terms taken directly from Arabic or, in the case of languages on the periphery, from the language which has served as a cultural carrier, for example, the Persian vocabulary in the languages of India, Pakistan and South East Asia. But, in these latter cases, the transplanting of basic vocabulary came about naturally and organically, rather as Latin vocabulary entered all the languages of Christian Europe. The situation is very different in moving from Arabic to, say, English and the solution needs to be thought out with care.

The answer to the lexicographical problem would appear to be two-fold: firstly, where necessary, to translate via a third language — for example, to translate Arabic into Thai, if this should ever be necessary, via English; and, secondly, to organize matters in such a way that the process of translation could be combined with that of lexicography in order to ensure both the standardization of terminology and the gradual production of new dictionaries where they are needed. This would, of course, require the active co-operation of translators and the establishment of some sort of central body or academy — of a 'school' of translation in fact.

Methods of Translation

There have been traditionally two main categories of translation and two main methods which, in a sense, correspond to them. These categories are: a) literal translations intended principally as a guide to the original, and aiming at no literary merit in their own right; and b) literary translations for the purposes of persons who have no interest in or linguistic access to, the original and which are intended to stand as readable and elegant texts in their own right. In practice, the two categories are often confused and sometimes justifiably so when the contiguity of languages or the particular skill of the translator enable literal and exact translation to be combined with elegance. In other historical cases, the cultural importance of texts rendered literally into a kind of 'translationese' has given birth to entirely new literary genres in the languages into which the translation is made, particularly if the original language enjoys overwhelming cultural prestige.

The two main methods of translation are: a) translation by committee, which can be very suitable for literal translation; and b) translation by individuals which is, on the whole, more conducive to literary and elegant translation. However, there are certain very outstanding exceptions to this; the King James Version of the Bible was produced by committee, and is yet unmatched for beauty of style in the English language, and so was the Septuagint.

In any event, the choice of category has to be made at the outset, and it can only depend upon the purpose for which the work is intended. If it be intended to assist students to read the original, then a literal and exact translation is generally called for accompanied, if necessary, by grammatical notes and the text of the original. It can, if speed of production is important, be produced by a body of translators, provided that a co-ordinator be appointed to ensure consistency of terminology and style. The translation should never, however, be so literal as to be either incomprehensible or repellent, as sometimes happens when the translators are more skilled in the original tongue than in that into which they are translating — a not uncommon failing.

If, however, it be decided to produce a translation which will stand in its own right, being intended not simply for students of the original language but for a more general public — perhaps including non-Muslims whom one wishes to draw to Islam — then the following factors are, I think, relevant:

a) The translator should be a master of his native tongue, well-versed in its various literary modes, grammatical subtleties and expressive possibilities and aware of its strengths and weaknesses, and he should then translate only into his native tongue. No depth of knowledge of the original language will compensate for lack of feeling and sensibility as regards the language into which one is translating, whereas a comparative lack of real depth in the language from which he is translating can be compensated for by good dictionaries and the advice of experts.

b) If, for practical reasons, a translator be required to work into a tongue that is not native to him, even if this be a tongue in which he has received a large part of his education, then he must be prepared to submit his work for criticism and correction to an informed and sensitive native speaker of the tongue into which he is translating. (There are, I know, certain outstanding exceptions in the past to this rule that a man should write in, or translate into, his native language alone — and in our own day too — but they remain exceptions, and the best of them have not hesitated to submit themselves to this discipline.)

c) In any case, and whatever his qualifications in the languages he is translating from and into, a translator should ideally be a man of virtue and some humility, for he is required to retain his linguistic and literary sensibility on the one hand and, on the other, to sacrifice his own ego to the point of faithfully transmitting ideas from one medium to another without imposing his own notions or mental colouring; and this is not always easy. Reshaping according to the exigencies of different languages is one thing, and distortion is another. It is for this reason that a translation is always best checked by a second person having appropriate qualifications in both subject and languages and also because men are fallible and can omit or mistranslate passages from sheer tiredness, for serious translation is demanding work.

d) A translator should, ideally, be well-versed in, and preferably favourably disposed towards, the subject with which he is dealing.

e) A translator, having if possible the above qualifications, should first of all familiarize himself with the entire work which he hopes to translate; then, taking into account the style, quality and historical period of the original, he should decide on an appropriate form of language for translation and adhere to it consistently. In order to be able to do this, he should know the purpose for which the translation is intended; if specialized knowledge or terminology is involved he should read existing works on the same subject and learn from them.

f) If he has time, he should first produce a translation that aims at the greatest possible fidelity to the original, and this is not, of course, necessarily the most literal translation for it is not fidelity to translate a beautiful original into an ugly reproduction in a second language in the pretended interests of exactitude; he should then check the whole and have it checked; then produce a polished, final version from his first one and do so — again if time allows — only after a lapse of time in which he has been able to free his mind from the idiom of the original, for this almost inevitably imposes itself to the detriment of the style of translation. Paradoxically, this is particularly true when the two languages are closely related, for one is lulled into a false sense of security.

g) Poetry presents a special case, for only a poet, or a person with an intense feeling for poetry in his own tongue, can hope to do it justice and such a person is not necessarily qualified linguistically to fathom the poetry of another language. In this case, it is better for translator and poet to work together, the one exploring and expounding the meaning and the other reshaping it as verse in his native tongue.

h) Finally, all that has been said in the preceding subparagraphs could be qualified by saying that translators who are both qualified in the original tongue and have a reasonable mastery of their own language are not very numerous and that, if any large scale programme of translation is to be attempted, collaboration between pairs of persons — the one a master of the original and the other a master of his own tongue — is a viable method, provided each give the other his due.

Conclusion

In the above remarks I have dealt only with general problems and matters of principle. If I have given very few examples of concrete problems, this is because, in fact, each task of translation produces its own difficulties and dilemmas and each has to be tackled quite separately in the light of general principles.

In insisting upon the innate nobility of human speech and the need to use language of the greatest possible dignity and lucidity in translating religious subjects, I have in mind one very real danger that is inherent when an attempt is made to work on an ambitiously large scale in order to counter secularizing tendencies; this is the danger of succumbing to the temptation of demeaning popularization and of modernization beyond the bounds of what is needed. Its inevitable concomitant is the degradation of language and, as a European, I can assure you that it is very widespread in the West, not least in the context of modern works on religion and in the field of translation from sacred and noble texts, and that it is extremely damaging.

I must turn finally to the items mentioned in the memorandum under the heading *Translation*, and try to comment briefly on them in the light of general principles.

a) The question of translating new textbooks is not so much a question for a translator as for their writers. Provided the books are sound in their contents and well written, there is no special problem; the only difficult question is whether a textbook written in a local language, with local requirements in mind, would necessarily be valid for other areas. In order to counter the deleterious effect of modern, Westernizing education, new textbooks are certainly required, but I venture to believe that only the main guidelines should be laid down centrally and that the task of producing the actual books should be left to the local authorities. It should not be forgotten that the centralizing and unifying and truth-bearing realities of Islam are contained in the Holy Qurān, the *Ḥadīth*, the treatises of the Schools of Law (*madhāhib*) and the writings of the great Saints and '*ulamā*' and that nothing can supplant them. If, however, to meet present exigencies, new textbooks are produced, the question of translating them must surely depend upon the merits of each, considered separately.

b) To establish a permanent bureau of translation is certainly a good idea if its main purpose be to ensure the high quality of translations, the standardization of terminology and the production of dictionaries and grammar books where they are needed. However, it could well run the risk of excessive centralization and unwieldiness and of sacrificing quality to quantity — the almost inevitable result of mass production. Again I would suggest rather the creation of an academy to set standards, define guidelines, offer advice, produce dictionaries and other reference works, and, if possible, assist the work of translation financially. It is probably impractical to bring all the translators together in one spot, and a translator can probably work best in his own country where his work can be directed by local authorities having local requirements in mind but, like the translators themselves, keeping their minds open to the suggestions and advice of the Academy.

c) An implementation centre, with the functions suggested in the memorandum, is an excellent idea, but these functions could well be subsumed by an academy of the type proposed above or, alternately, the two should work together in the closest possible collaboration.

d) The translation of the Holy Qurān poses innumerable subtle and delicate questions; I have already touched upon some of these.

My final, tentative conclusion must be that in order to withstand the corrosive effects on Islamic life of Westernization and Westernized concepts, in education as in other fields, it is nor enough — and indeed it is not befitting — simply to accept certain Western and modern premises and then, as it were, to attempt somehow to 'Islamicize' them or to 'modernize' Islam. All that is necessary to ensure the preservation and integrity of the Islamic way of life is contained in the Holy Qurān and the Traditions of the Blessed Prophet — on whom be Blessings and Peace — in the codifications of the Schools of Law and in the writings of the great Saints. It is a question, primarily, of their intelligent and pious application and, thus, of bringing them to the urgent attention of all.

In this, translation can — and must — play a great part where access to these inestimable gifts of Divine Providence is barred by linguistic barriers. But its primary purpose must be to lead people — or to lead them back — to the originals, particularly in the case of the Holy Qurān, and to first principles. In this, there are many languages that have a role to play, including the English language. But the main emphasis — or, at the very least, a commensurate emphasis — must be placed on the improved teaching of Arabic, the language of Divine Revelation, and on the preservation everywhere in *Dār al-Islām* of its script. 'And God Knoweth best.'

Chapter Seven

The Teaching of Arabic in the Non-Arabic Speaking Muslim World: Present Conditions and Possibilities with Reference to the Desirable Ideal

Seyyed Muhammad Yusuf

Born 1916, Pakistani; Died 1978; M.A. Ph.D. (Arabic), M.A. (Punjab), B. Theology, Aligarh Muslim University, Aligarh, India; Professor of Arabic, Karachi University from 1959 until his death; Professor, National University of Malaysia, Kuala Lumpur, 1974–75; Head of the Department of Arabic, University of Ceylon 1953–59; Lecturer, Institute of Oriental Languages, Fuad I University, Cairo, 1947–53, Lecturer, Muslim University, Aligarh, India, 1942–47; publications include: *Kitāb al-ashbāh wa'l-naẓā'ir li'lkhālidiyyīn*, Cairo, 1958–65; *Al-Arabiyyak Lughat-al-Qur'ān*, Rabat, 1969; *Some Aspects of Islamic Culture*, Lahore, 1961; *Studies in Islamic History and Culture*, Lahore, 1970, *Economic Justice in Islam*, Lahore, 1972; Urdu Translation: Al-Sakhāwī *Al-tanbīh wa'l-tawbīkh*, Lahore, 1968, Ibn Ṭufail's *Ḥayy B. Yaqẓān*, Lahore, 1961.

1 The Organic Relationship between the Arabic Language and Islam

A study of history would prove that but for Islam the Arabic language would never have spread to various parts of the world and would have never remained and flourished as a living language. Instead it would have declined and died out as a living language like Sanskrit, Greek or Latin. It may be trite to say that it was only Islam which united the Arabs and enabled them to establish a great power which had a profound influence inside and outside the Arabian Peninsula. Even if they had been only zealous nationalists or fanatical racists driven by their pre-Islamic chauvinism to conquer their neighbours the Persians, the Romans, the Copts, the Berbers, the Negroes, and the Goths, the Arabs would not have been able to force so many foreign nations to give up their languages and use Arabic in their homes, markets, temples, schools and offices, or more than that, become Arabicized in their thinking, interests, emotions, literature, arts and customs.

The attempts of colonialists and imperialists which Muslims have seen and from which they have suffered in modern times prove the futility of compulsion in trying to introduce an alien language. Western powers invaded many countries and conquered by force nations of various races and religions, but failed in their blatant attempts to exterminate the native languages of the conquered and replace them in public life by those of their own. All they could achieve was the creation by promises and threats of a particular class of sycophants and toadies. That class of people blindly adopted a foreign culture alien to the elements of their origin, personality and background and consequently lived in emotional isolation, arrogantly cut off from their natural roots in a national, religious and moral environment. Although they still constitute a very small proportion of the total population in every Muslim country concerned, this élite still uses the foreign language for special purposes and occasions. Thus a student of history should draw lessons from how Arabic spread from Iraq to Andalusia after the emergence of Islam. Such a study would easily conclude that Islam attracted the people so strongly to the Holy Qurān and its language that they voluntarily became Arabicized. The fact that non-Arabs contributed a great deal to the field of the teaching of Arabic, through their study of the linguistic sciences, is further evidence. We are indeed indebted to the Holy Qurān alone for the survival of classical Arabic and the continual use of its flawless form in spoken and written communication until the present time, thanks to God's promise 'We have, without doubt, sent down the Message, and We will assuredly guard it from corruption'. Arabic has not declined, perished, or faded away into only colloquial dialects.

2 Arab-Muslim and Non-Arab Muslim Societies: The Differences and the Common Factor Between Them

There are two categories of Muslim nations. The first category comprises the nations which have completely given up their original native languages in favour of Arabic for the purposes of everyday life. The second category comprises the nations which have given Arabic special attention because it is the language of the Holy Qurān and the Muslim religion. They have also established it as the language of their literature and science and the medium of education in schools. Arabic has therefore become the main element in the culture of the second category, and although it is not used for the purposes of everyday life in the homes and shops, it has limited the native languages to these areas, and completely taken over the field of science, literature and education. Even when local languages developed as years went by and started to creep into the courts and government offices, or apologetically tried to reach the field of poetry and other literary genres, they never hoped to acquire the status of independent languages, but always attached themselves to Arabic and orbited round it. The public revered Arabic more than any language, and the élite found it indispensable for religion, general culture, science and literature.

The difference between the Arab and non-Arab Muslim societies, therefore, lies in the use of Arabic. While it is used in the first category as the language of speech for the purposes of everyday life, it is not used for the same purposes in the second. However, the common factor between both categories is the fact that their societies are based on Islamic law (*Sharī'ah*). This factor logically and practically requires the establishment of a unified system of education based on Islamic studies and the Islamic language (not only the 'first' or the 'original' but the 'only'), and that is Arabic, the language of the Holy Qurān and the Blessed Prophet's Traditions.

3 Enforcement of Islamic Law Is The Conerstone of a Muslim Environment

A Muslim environment cannot exist without the enforcement of Islamic Law (*Sharī'ah*). If Islamic Law is not observed, what is left of Islam will be only the outer shape or form which can be seen in religious observances and rites. Consequently, Muslims will not feel the need for studying Islamic Law. This is the reason why Islamic studies are declining and stagnating in Arab and non-Arab countries, and why no attention is paid to the Arabic language in non-Arab Muslim countries at present. Why should any attention be paid to Islamic and Arabic studies if the law enforced in almost all the Muslim countries is unfortunately, a foreign positive law? Is it not true that most Muslim countries enforce only a very small part of Islamic Law, and that is the personal statutes? The courses on Islamic Law which are studied in those countries are purely theoretical courses which do not emphasize the existence of an Islamic environment, but rather make students feel it does not exist outside their lecture rooms.

There has been a great deal of discussion about using the cinema, television and radio to create an Islamic environment, but this is the same as putting the cart before the horse. How can Muslims subject machines and systems to the service of Islam before subjecting themselves, their thought and work, to Islamic Law?

4 Facts about the Position of the Arabic Language in Islamic Education and Culture in Non-Arab Muslim Countries through History up to the 19th Century A.D.

a) The Arabic language enjoyed absolute supremacy in the educational curricula because Islamic Law prevailed in the life of Muslim peoples. They referred to it in all their social dealings, business transactions, and government decisions in peace and war.

b) The Arabic language maintained its absolute supremacy and never had to face competition from local languages. After the emergence of local languages literary genres were written in them and some subjects were translated into them, but this was done only for the benefit of the uneducated and half-educated majority, not out of respect for the local languages or because the educated people or the scholars thought they could substitute the local languages for Arabic. Arabic kept its supremacy in the educational curricula of non-Arab Muslim countries, and the local languages were content to be in a subordinate position. That was only natural and in the interest of the local languages themselves.

c) No foreign language, such as English or French, was imposed by force on Muslims. Consequently there was no chance for the development of duality in thought and behaviour in politics, government or social customs.

5 The Present Situation Indicates Imminent Disaster

Everything followed that natural course for centuries until Muslims were afflicted by Western occupation. Then everything was turned upside-down. Discussion here is confined to the factors that considerably affected the position of the Arabic language. The most important of these factors are:

a) The substitution of positive (foreign) law for Islamic Law.
b) The introduction of a foreign educational system (English/French) and its establishment by colonialist means. The danger of this factor lies in the following:
   i. The secularization of education in the sense that Islamic Law (*Sharī'ah*) is no longer the nucleus of all educational curricula.
   ii. Deposing Arabic from its throne and imposing the supremacy of foreign lanugage on education, thought, ways of life, government administration, international communications, and commercial and industrial affairs.
c) Sowing the seeds of limited nationalism which competes with the feeling of Muslim fraternity and causes the Muslim World to disintegrate. One of the clear manifestations of nationalism is the pride taken by Arab countries in their respective colloquial dialects rather than in classical Arabic, and by non-Arab Muslim countries in their local languages rather than in Arabic (the Arabs' language). A logical extension of this nationalistic trend is the suggestion that the Arabic script should be replaced by the Romanized alphabet.

One of the common misconceptions is that colonialism killed the local languages or was hostile to them in non-Arab Muslim countries. The truth is that it was colonialism which spread the idea of 'The Mother Tongue', sponsored the local languages, and even flattered and encouraged them to compete with Arabic (and Persian too). It was also colonialism which attempted to glorify colloquial dialects and revive Berber and other languages thereby destroying classical Arabic in the Arab countries. As a result of those attempts, Urdu, for instance, gained momentum during British rule and replaced Arabic and Persian in the cultural aspects of life, although it has not been able yet to remove English from its place. The same thing happened with local languages in other non-Arab muslim countries.

As it was not practicable to try and persuade the Muslim people in any country, Arab or non-Arab, to give up their religion completely, the rise of local languages made non-Arab Muslims more interested in Quranic translations than in the original Arabic. This breakaway from Arabic has been gaining strength to the extent that it is now blatantly and insolently suggested that local languages should be used for calling for prayers (*adhān*) and for performing prayers themselves (*ṣalāt*).

What is even more serious is that since independence from Western domination Arabic has not been used in religious education. A new subject called 'Islamic Studies' has been introduced into the modern curricula of state schools and colleges. That subject is based on a collection of English or local language translations, perhaps inadequate and not approved, of some Quranic chapters and the Blessed Prophet's Traditions. The new subject also includes comparisons between Islam and some of the modern philosophical and economic ideologies (without involving a thorough and complete study of Islam). Comparisons are sometimes so invalid and biased that they make young students feel that the Islamic religion is deficient and needs something from outside to complete or perfect it.

Here are a few of the semi-political phenomena which exemplify the deviation of education and culture from the true Arabic tradition in non-Arab Muslim countries:

Turkey

Turkey was the first Islamic country to substitute the Latin script for the Arabic script, to prohibit the use of Arabic in the calls for prayers and to sever all relations between Turkish and Arabic to the extent that Arabic words have been eliminated from Turkish or reduced to the minimum possible, and Arabic itself is not taught any more even as a foreign language (because it will never be a foreign language). Whatever is said now to the effect that the situation is improving and that new trends have recently appeared, the sad fact remains that Arabic is still excluded from the national curricula and the general culture of the faithful and brave Turkish people.

Iran

A wave of 'Pure Persian' swept over Iran for a short period but it was quickly broken by the solid rock of reality which stood fast against extreme currents, and 'Pure Persian' soon faded away. It is only fair to state that scholars and writers in Iran recovered their senses and were wise enough to admit the importance of the Arabic elements in the Persian language. The situation in Iran is, therefore, much better than it is in other non-Arab Muslim countries. Arabic is actually a compulsory subject for all the arts students in Iran up to the highest level of study.

Pakistan

This young country was founded on the basis of Islam and Muslim fraternity. However, it soon became culturally barren and was then an easy prey to nationalism disguised as Islam. The effect was an enthusiasm for Urdu as an Islamic language. One may think that this enthusiasm was motivated by Islamic feelings and that the enthusiasts aimed their attacks at English which dominated all the intellectual and administrative fields, but the truth is that the protagonists of Urdu were keen supporters of English. They frequently stressed that the status of English as a respectable and compulsory language should not be affected. They did not say a word about Arabic, but they kept watch to prevent Arabic from occupying the position it deserves as the first language in the state education curricula, because they realized that Urdu would not stand competition with Arabic, and that whenever and wherever Urdu was used it would only be subordinate to Arabic. They knew that Arabic is a sacred language, rich in material, easy to inflect and suitable for all scientific purposes.

Moreover, the protagonists of Urdu had received their education in English and had no knowledge of Arabic at all. Their enthusiasm for Urdu as an Islamic language (against Arabic) was only a clever but malicious trick. The truth was revealed when a suggestion by the late Aga Khan the Third to establish Arabic as the first language in Pakistan, was absolutely rejected although it was supported by many valid arguments. The protagonists of Urdu rose against the Aga Khan, and let English watch the victory of Islamic Urdu (as the extremists call it) over Arabic. But that was only a short-lived victory, because Urdu nationalism soon met with the same fate as the Arabs met when they revolted against the Turks. Fighting broke out between supporters of Urdu and supporters of other local languages such as Bengali and Sindhi, and blood was shed in every street and alley. When the battles were over, monuments were erected all over the country in memory of the Bengali and Urdu 'martyrs' who fought and were killed in the name of ignorant enthusiasm. The monuments are still there and admirers continue to visit them on special occasions and pay homage to the 'martyrs' by putting flowers on them, just as the pagans used to do. In the meantime, the '*ulamā*', who are the heirs of the prophets, kept silent, and even when they were asked about the issue just mumbled and gave no clear answer. The politically minded Muslims were also cautious and scared of the strong opposition at the time. It is not surprising then that Arabic stays forgotten and neglected. No wonder it has no supporters or martyrs. Needless to say the situation has not changed very much after the Islamic Summit Conference at Lahore, and the introduction of a clause in the Pakistan constitution concerning the responsibility of the government towards the popularization of Arabic. Arabic is still as neglected in state schools, colleges and universities as it was before the conference.

Bangladesh

The feverish Bengali fanaticism has been mentioned earlier in this report. It should be added here that that fanaticism was mainly aimed at Urdu after it had become a symbol of the supremacy of Western Pakistanis including the Muslim immigrants from India. Arabic, however, was completely forgotten except when it was suggested that the Arabic script could be used for writing Bengali in place of the Indian characters. Even that suggestion was unfortunately rejected. Arabic seemed to have lost all respect and to have no other value than its graphemes which are used for writing Urdu. It is certainly common knowledge now that the Bengali versus Urdu case was the beginning of a political movement which ended with the intervention of India and her ally Russia to separate the Eastern part of Pakistan. Now that Bangladesh has become an independent state (independent of Pakistan certainly) the only languages used are Bengali and English. It is not important which of them enjoys supremacy in education and culture. What concerns us is that Arabic is still neglected. The language is neither used for communication, nor are its graphemes used for writing Bengali.

South East Asia, including Indonesia and Malaysia

This part of the world used to be a field of many Arab activities as a result of which Arabic was spoken by a considerable number of its population; Arabic letters were used for writing the Indonesian and Malay languages; and the literature of both languages was influenced by Arabic literature. That was the state of affairs until the emergence of the republican and democratic régimes which, for the sake of the Muslim majority, had to give up some elements of Muslim culture just to secure the approval of the non-Muslim minority. Indonesia, followed by Malaysia, substituted the Latin for the Arabic script, and both gave their respective local languages (vernaculars) so respectable a status that they competed with Arabic in education and culture.

There are some well-established Arabic schools which are recognized and admired by Al-Azhar University. All the Islamic subjects are taught in Arabic in those schools but whenever the government concerned turns its attention to those schools and attempts to carry out a reform which aims at making religious education more suited to the modern age, as it is alleged, the position of Arabic becomes even weaker, for two reasons:

a) Modern subjects are extended at the expense of Islamic subjects.
b) What is more serious, the local language competes with Arabic

even in the teaching of Islamic subjects. This trend is very obvious in modern universities, where there are separate departments, or even colleges of Islamic Studies; but the use of the local language is continually growing, whereas Arabic is increasingly confined to the study of a few texts.

The appropriate use of Arabic in Islamic culture and education is mainly hindered by a class of people who have received a modern, foreign education and were trained by the colonizers to succeed them in government and administration. That class seized the opportunity after the independence of the non-Arab Muslim countries, and exploited their authority and influence by talking about Islam. Their talk was full of inaccuracies, fabrications and irrelevant quotations. They were not even ashamed of talking about Islam although they did not know a letter of Arabic. Some of them were lawyers who studied Roman, English, French and Swiss law, but never studied Arabic, the Holy Qurān, or the Blessed Prophet's Traditions, and yet they spoke about Islamic Law in local and international meetings. Others were historians who studied the history of the world but never studied Islamic history, yet still talked about the history of Islam and quoted secondary sources which did not help them to pronounce the Arabic names correctly. Those who have received foreign education in the non-Arab Muslim countries frequently refer to English translations of the Holy Qurān, look for English translations of the Blessed Prophet's Traditions, and absorb information about Islam and Islamic Law from English, French and other foreign language publications (mostly produced by Western Orientalists whose animosity towards Islam has been proved beyond any doubt). Such people as these claim there is no need for Arabic, despise others who study Islam from its original Arabic sources, and try hard to divorce Arabic from programmes of Islamic studies — if any. This attitude is a blatant violation of the sanctity of the Islamic religion and an attack on scholarly values. The situation has even reached the stage, particularly in Pakistan and India, where those without any knowledge of Arabic see no harm in translating the Holy Qurān and its exegesis. Dr. Bint al-Shāṭi' protested very strongly against this trend during her visit to India. She wrote in the *Al-Ahrām* newspaper calling upon governments and scholars to exert all the influence they could to protect the Holy Qurān 'from the abuse of translators, the mistakes of interpreters, and the aggression of adapters.'

The class of people receiving a foreign education are those who send young inexperienced Muslims to European and American universities to study the Holy Qurān, Islamic traditions, Islamic jurisprudence and history. Their tutors in those universities are mostly Jewish and Christian missionaries who in most cases work as advisors to their respective ministries of foreign affairs and intelligence services. Even when the subject of study is Arabic literature, students from the non-Arab Muslim countries are forced, in European and American universities, to learn German and French as requisites for obtaining higher degrees in Arabic literature, while Arabic itself is completely neglected. No wonder the Muslim students' knowledge of Arabic deteriorates after their study abroad.

More harm is done if the students of orientalists take teaching jobs. They reflect distorted views, in addition to displaying their chronic weakness in Arabic and their ignorance of original Islamic sources. Dr. Mohammad Iqbal long ago warned young Muslims against the attraction of studying Islamic subjects under orientalists and advised them instead to seek the scholarly teaching of faithful Muslim Sheikhs in Egypt and other Arab Muslim countries.

There are two distinct methods of studying Arabic in the non-Arab Muslim countries:

The first is predominant in old schools. The teaching of Arabic is always associated in these schools with the teaching of Islamic subjects such as Quranic exegesis, Islamic traditions, and jurisprudence. As a result of this close relationship, Arabic language and literature are not studied for their own sake, but only as a means of learning Islamic subjects. The literature syllabus, therefore, has not changed in those schools for centuries, and such titles as *Maqāmāt al-ḥarīrī*, *Ḥamāsah Abī Tammām*, and '*al-Sab'ah mu'allaqāt*' have been read by generation after generation. All the emphasis is put on teaching the rules of inflection and sentence structure through the use of dull and boring examples about Zayd and 'Amr, but very little reading is practised and very few exercises are given. The product of this syllabus is a student who knows the rules of morphology and syntax and memorizes a number of vocabulary items which help him understand the meaning of Holy Qurān chapters and traditions, but nothing else. He does not know anything about the different styles of Arabic, does not develop a literary taste or an ability to criticize prose and poetry, and does not develop the skills or writing, public speaking or even normal everyday speaking in Arabic. All these skills and abilities are beyond his reach because he is never interested in literature for its own sake.

A group of scholars suggested in the last century the reformation of that part of the method in the old schools. As a result of this movement the *Dārul 'Ulūm Nadwat al-'Ulamā'* was opened in Lucknow (India). The required results were achieved as far as writing, journalism and public speaking are concerned, but scientific research in literature still needs more attention. The same can be said about similar schools in Pakistan such as the Arab-Muslim School in Near Town (Karachi) where its Principal, Shaykh Muhammad Yūsuf al-Binnūrī, is making special efforts to improve the study of literature.

It is worth mentioning that spoken Arabic is very easy for much of the population in South East Asia. This may be due to the fact that some Arab communities have settled there and the fact that they have maintained strong and permanent relations with Al-Azhar. Nevertheless, very few South-East Asians are interested in Arabic literature. The case is reversed in India and Pakistan where some students of Arabic have made valuable contributions to its literature, although the general standard of spoken Arabic for everyday purposes is very low.

The second method is predominant in the modern Westernized colleges and universities. This method is designed so that language and literature are studied for their own sake without being associated with Islamic religious studies. The latter had been neglected and ostracized from modern universities until very recently. When Islamic Studies was introduced into modern universities just before or just after independence, the current of nationalism was at its strongest, as a result of which Islamic subjects were studied in the local languages supported by English in some cases instead of Arabic, which was not known by those responsible for organizing education. The main point is that Arabic language and literature are studied for their own sake as part of the language and literature courses and completely independent of the religious subjects written in Arabic.

Classical languages, led by Arabic, used to enjoy a coveted position in modern education programmes during English rule. Arabic had the same status as Greek and Latin have in Europe. Even Persian was not thought of as independent of Arabic. Local languages were treated as new branches of Arabic and Persian. That was only natural from both the historical and the purely scientific points of view. After independence the current of nationalism swept Arabic away from its coveted position and left it in the cold. It became neither compulsory (the study of one classical language—Arabic, Persian or Sanskrit—was a compulsory subject up to B.A. level during British rule), nor attractive enough to be chosen voluntarily. The local languages, on the other hand, (usually referred to as the 'National' languages in the West out of respect and glorification) jumped to the top position and became compulsory subjects. It was even claimed that Arabic in particular was not necessary although it was agreed that it should coexist with English as another compulsory subject. In the end Arabic was completely eliminated from the fields of study where it is indispensable, namely, religious subjects, Islamic history, and Islamic philosophy.

After independence, however, departments of Arabic in the modern colleges and universities kept on trying to do their job properly. The academic atmosphere in these institutions was favourable to changing the syllabi with a view to reviving and propagating the old Arab legacy. New subjects such as the history of literature, principles of literary criticism, Spanish literature and modern literature, have therefore been introduced in them. (Compare these with the rigid syllabus of the old schools which are confined to the exclusive study of certain textbooks). The new syllabi produce graduates who have studied different kinds of literature in depth and understood the influence of social change and literary trends of creative works. They have also developed literary taste to a certain degree, and learned modern methods of research and investigation. Nevertheless, they have acquired neither adequate mastery in speaking or writing Arabic, nor full mastery of morphological and syntactic rules which would enable them to read correctly and fluently. It has been noticed that most of the research papers and thesis submitted to the universities for obtaining higher degrees in Arabic language and literature are written in English, which is the language traditionally used for that purpose in Western universities. It is only recently that papers and theses submitted to some Indian and Pakistan universities have been written in Arabic. *al-Turk fīmu'allafāt al-Jāḥiẓ* (*The Turks in the Works of al-Jāḥiẓ*) which has been published in book form by *Dār-al-thaqāfah* in Beirut, is an example of a thesis written in Arabic. It was submitted to the Department of Arabic, University of Karachi, which approved it and conferred a Doctor's degree upon the applicant.

Suggestions

In the light of the previous discussion of the historical background and the present situation, the following suggestions are made:

(1) Since Arabic is the main element in Islamic religion and culture, the governments of non-Arab Muslim countries are called on to take measures immediately for the establishment of Arabic as the first language of all their Muslim population. According to Imām al-Shāfi'ī, 'Everybody who can learn Arabic must do so, for it is the first language' (quoted by Salafī). The first language, in this context, does not mean the official language used for administration, or the spoken language used for everyday purposes; it means that Arabic should come first before the *local* vernacular (national) language and any foreign language (English and others) in education and general culture, so that nobody could be described as truly educated unless he learned Arabic and acquired mastery in using it.

(2) Following the establishment of Arabic as the first language, all local languages should be written in the Arabic script. Governments and leaders seeking the friendship of the West should reinstate the Arabic script, having realized the religious and cultural loss suffered as a result of using the Latin instead of the Arabic script in writing their languages.

These two measures, namely establishing the primacy of Arabic in education and the use of the Arabic script in writing all local languages (vernaculars) of the non-Arab Muslim countries, would certainly direct the local languages on to an Arab-Muslim path. Consequently every educated person, poet or prose writer, would speak two languages— Arabic and his vernacular. The meeting of both languages in one culture would let the old spring of Arabic flow again, as it used to in the past, and supply the local languages with words, structures, technical terms, figures of speech, thoughts, ideas, and forms of poetry and prose writing. Those springs have dried up since educated people abandoned Arabic and took up English or other European languages.

A study of Persian, Turkish and Urdu would show that they are clearly influenced by Arabic. Examples of this influence are:

(i) A large number of words — 60% or more in some cases — nouns, adjectives, verbs and their derivations, are borrowed from Arabic.

(ii) Religious and technical terms and scientific and literary expressions are either borrowed or translated from Arabic.

(iii) Literary genres in those three languages are similar to Arabic literary genres.

The metre, caesura and even themes of poetry are only a few examples. Such a close relationship as this was developed between Arabic and the local languages because the writers had learnt Arabic as the supreme language, and therefore borrowed from it to fertilize their vernaculars and develop them so that they could serve Islamic religion and culture. This happened in varying degrees with all local languages spoken by Muslims in all parts of the world. The cause is the same; the effect varies only in degree.

The importance of these two measures is stressed because they are essential for restoring the important status of Arabic in national education programmes in non-Arab Muslim countries. Both steps pave the way for the third suggestion:

(3) The replacement of Arabic by the local languages or English in teaching Islamic religious subjects, which is prevalent in non-Arab Muslim countries, should be strongly discouraged. Such an attitude conflicts with religious purposes and purely scientific values. All circles concerned should take steps to see that the situation is changed and all the Islamic subjects are taught in Arabic only, at all levels of education. Exceptions could be made in primary and secondary schools and the children at these stages could be given simple religious education courses in the vernacular which is familiar to them and easily understood. When they move on to higher education students should be trained in reading with understanding and in studying the Arabic texts.

The religious subjects are: Holy Qurān, the Blessed Prophet's Traditions, exegesis, the authentication of Traditions, Islamic jurisprudence, and the sources. These are the primary religious subjects which should not and cannot be taught except through Arabic texts.

There are also secondary subjects which require a knowledge of Arabic in order to make it possible consult original Arabic sources even if they are not studied exclusively through Arabic texts. These subjects are Islamic history and philosophy, if they are studied (not as special subjects) as part of the history of the world or general philosophy. The same applies to the study of personal statutes as part of general law. The latter is a foreign positive non-Islamic law still enforced in many Arab and non-Arab Muslim countries even after the end of political colonization.

If Arabic is to be given a worthy position and due respect in comparison with the local languages, English and other foreign languages — which are still competing with Arabic, fighting it and trying to replace it in national education programmes, even after independence — then the following steps should be taken to correct the faults in the present situation:

First: Students who finish courses at the private religious Arabic schools spend many years learning Arabic by the old 'grammar-translation' method which until very recently was also followed in teaching foreign languages, particularly the old classical languages in Europe. This method produces students who know the morphology and syntax of the language and can understand the texts they read, but it does not provide for the following:

(a) The development of a reasonable mastery of the written and spoken language so that students can use it in composition and creative writing and in public speaking and everyday communication.

(b) A wide reading of old literary texts.

(c) The introduction of modern literary works which were completely neglected in their courses.

(d) The study of the history of literature and the political and social background which influenced it.

(e) The study of the principles and methods of literary criticism.

The main factor that causes these deficiencies — apart from the old teaching method — is the absence of an environment which motivates the student and even forces him to use and practise, in real life situations, the linguistic material he learns at school. The worst effect of the absence of a favourable environment is the pronunciation of Arabic with a local accent which does not follow correct patterns of rhythm and intonation. This applies to India and Pakistan; but in South East Asia pronunciation of Arabic is closer to authentic Arabic. Oddly enough, this may be due to the fact that since there is a large number of Arabic words in Urdu and their meanings have been altered and pronunciation distorted, semantic and syntactic mistakes occur frequently. On the other hand, Muslims in South East Asia have paid special attention to teaching the reading of the Holy Quran and its recital by Arab teachers in all the cities and villages, and consequently they have developed an almost authentic Arabic pronunciation.

(4) As the main objective should be the creation of an Arabic environment, priority should be given to creating colleges/schools in Arab countries and to designing special courses for students of religious Arabic schools in other countries. Such courses should be for one or two years, and their syllabuses should include the following:

(a) Practice in pronunciation and the reading of texts, and lessons in Quranic recitation.
(b) Practice in public speaking, creative writing, and composition.
(c) Extensive and comprehensive studies of old literary works.
(d) Study of modern literature.
(e) History of Arabic literature.
(f) Literary criticism.

It is hoped that students trained in a really Arabic environment will be able, on return to their home countries, to offer valuable help in raising the standard of Arabic and popularizing its teaching. These students need to concentrate on classical Arabic, and should not waste their time on local dialects.

Second: Graduates of departments of Arabic in modern universities also suffer from the absence of an Arabic environment. Their plight is even worse because, generally speaking, they do not achieve a high standard in theoretical or practical morphology and syntax. On the other hand, university graduates are more knowledgeable and widely read in classical literature. They also study modern literature as a separate subject, and are familiar with the principles of literary criticism.

(5) These graduates then need the same kind of college in Arab countries, with syllabi to suit their special circumstances, and should be separated from the other students for specialized subjects.

It is strongly recommended that governments and local authorities should give teachers in Arabic schools, as well as in modern and traditional colleges and universities, the opportunity to join such proposed colleges and after receiving advanced practical training, implement the desirable reforms in Arabic language teaching programmes. Unified teacher training will probably produce correspondingly unified teaching programmes in Arabic language and literature. The achievement of such unification would prove significant in comparison with previous failures to save the Muslim nations from duality in education, thought and action.

The measures suggested for popularizing Arabic in non-Arabic Muslim countries are given below in order of priority. The first priority should be raising the status of Arabic in national education programmes, by training teachers and giving them the opportunity to reform these programmes and lay a new sound foundation for Arabic within the national frameworks.

Once this measure is taken at school level, the next step is to teach those educated adults who have left school or finished their education without taking any courses in Arabic. These adults can be divided into two categories: those who wish to learn Arabic for practical reasons such as taking jobs, or living in Arab countries, and those who wish to learn Arabic to read religious and literary material.

People in the first category are in most cases highly qualified people in such fields as medicine, engineering and banking. An increasing number has been emigrating to Arab countries since the oil income of these countries increased. Learning Arabic for practical purposes should be encouraged by both the Arab employers and the foreign Muslim employees. Although knowledge of the host country's language would certainly increase the efficiency of the employee, it would also have other valuable effects and create stronger bonds between different parts of the Muslim world. Arabization and Islam always went hand in hand in the early centuries of our history. The present situation is a result of colonialism but we are voluntarily changing to its legacy in our thought and culture. It is disgraceful that Muslims should communicate in such a foreign language as English, even in conferences held in the name of Muslim brotherhood to praise the originality of Muslim contributions. Some foreign Muslims have held key posts for many years in Arab countries and performed their duties most efficiently and conscientiously, but they stay foreigners in Arab circles because they do not know Arabic. Much is lost if the relationship between two Muslims is confined to work and payment only, and no opportunity is taken to use the ideal tool, Arabic, for exchanging ideas and cementing friendship so that formalities can be eliminated and closer ties established.

(6) Special schools for teaching Arabic to all those who apply for jobs in Arab countries should be opened in non-Arabic Muslim countries. However, the following points should be noted:

These applicants are highly qualified, educated and cultured people whose abilities have matured, including the ability to learn foreign languages such as English and French.

Consequently, the 'Direct Method' of teaching is not suitable. When a child learns a language from his mother he or she hears his mother saying words and sentences appropriate to certain situations; then he responds by imitating her speech. He does not care about rules or worry about inflection but stores the words he hears and repeats them in similar situations.

Learning is different for educated adults who are used to written rules for learning various subjects and foreign languages. It will be noticed that adult learners, such as university students, ask about the rules when they come across different case-endings, for example.

The method that suits educated adults is 'Cognitive Code Learning'.

Code learning helps the learner make progress from mere imitation to creative use of the language when he finds himself suddenly in a new situation he has never met before. Code learning is the key to transformational grammar, and it is natural for a mature person to possess this key. There is nothing monstrous about rules of grammar if they are well presented and explained by examples and the student is encouraged to discover the rules for himself by deduction. Linguistic rules are the same as for other natural phenomena in the universe. Natural sciences such as physics, botany and zoology are only attempts to discover God's creation and organization of natural phenomena. Arabic grammar has been truly described as a 'science' because its rules are as regular and as reliable as natural phenomena, contrary to most modern languages which are full of irregularities.

Grammar is not an end in itself, but a means to developing mastery of the language. Nevertheless, a student should be helped to identify the rules while he is listening to the repetition of examples or while he is reading texts which he fully understands.

Applicants for jobs in Arab countries, while employed in their home countries, usually cannot afford to take full-time courses in Arabic because of work and social commitments, and have to study it in their free time. They must, therefore, study Arabic for at least a year, during which they have to work hard to understand the structure of the language, and the simple rules of inflection and case-endings, and acquire the ability to understand easy texts and the ability to speak fluently for everyday usage.

Modern audio-visual aids, fashionable these days, are certainly very useful if they are used properly and not just as show-pieces from the West. It should be remembered that they are only 'aids' and that they can never replace the teacher who should still play the major rôle in the teaching process. There is no point in giving students records or tapes with model Arabic pronunciation if their teacher is producing the sounds incorrectly in a corrupt foreign accent.

Governments and local authorities in non-Arab Muslim countries ought to encourage applicants for jobs in Arab countries to learn Arabic, and provide them with facilities to do so.

(7) Partly educated people who wish to learn Arabic for religious and cultural purposes should be given special courses, adapted from the courses for job applicants in the same schools. It might be possible for this category to learn by radio or television in the comfort of their own homes. Lessons in this case should be of a general and simple type but should occasionally include individual teaching, drilling and testing. Radio and television courses could be jointly designed by Arab and local experts,

and are an obvious field where technical aid could be given by Arabs.

(8) It is recommended that Arab governments should send qualified teachers of Arabic to (a) the traditional schools, and (b) the modern universities in non-Arab Muslim countries. Some Arab countries have been doing this for some time, but in the light of past experience planners should consider the following points, bearing in mind that education, qualifications and attitudes should be the factors that determine the assignment of teachers to different educational institutions:

(a) Graduates of old colleges and universities such as Al-Azhar and its equivalents in other Arab countries should be sent to old-type schools in non-Arab Muslim countries.

(b) Modern university teachers who have Master's and Doctor's degrees should be sent to modern universities in non-Arab Muslim countries. It has been noticed that scholars from Al-Azhar and other old type institutions do not fit into the pattern of modern universities, and consequently do not achieve the aims set for them. This is not meant to belittle the old-type scholars, but harmony of attitudes and similarity of educational background can help to unite people from the same country.

(c) Primary or secondary school teachers should be sent to corresponding types of schools; otherwise they may suffer from various psychological problems, and the main aim will probably not be achieved. This is an objective criticism of what actually happens, and nobody should be ashamed of it.

(9) It would be very useful to open model Arabic schools at kindergarten, primary and secondary level similar to English schools that exist in large numbers in non-Arab Muslim countries at the moment. Children could be trained from an early age in such schools to use Arabic as the principal and popular language for conversation, public speaking, writing and instruction in other subjects.

Arab governments should undertake to open model schools incorporating the high standards of schools in non-Arab Muslim countries. The Arab contribution should be 70% and the local, 30% of the building and maintenance expenses involved while the administration of each school should be in the hands of a board on which both contributors are represented in equal numbers.

It is imperative that local authorities should participate with Arab countries and governments in every effort made to promote and popularize Arabic so that they do not evade or abandon their responsibility for the language. These local authorities bear the responsibility for, and pay special attention to, the teaching of English as a compulsory subject at all stages of education. They also allot a major part of the educational budget to science and technology. Should Arabic then be neglected, either to be supported by the Arabs, or to be alienated from Muslim societies because they are not Arab?

When Mohammad Ali Alloubah Pasha was the Egyptian Ambassador to Pakistan he suggested that Egypt should open Egyptian schools in Pakistan to teach Arabic. Even after he had resigned office he went on repeating his proposal in speeches he gave occasionally in the Pakistan Embassy in Cairo. Here is a quotation from one of his speeches, 'The Egyptian government has left Pakistan's hand stretched in the air and has not opened Egyptian schools in that country whose population is twice as big as the total population of the member states of the Arab League.'

Ustaz Abbas Khedr commented on this in the August 28th 1950 issue of the *al-Risālah* magazine as follows, 'The fact that the Pakistani government or its embassy in Cairo attaches great importance to that call indicates that it is taking the matter seriously. The Pakistani Government should be practical and build those schools in Pakistan, then send for teachers from different Arab countries to go and teach in them, not stretch its hand in the air.'

Certainly Mohammad Ali Alloubah Pasha was as sincere in his suggestion as Ustaz Abbas Khedr was serious in his comment on the duty of the local government in this respect. It is a duty which should not be abandoned, but in fact the governments of non-Arab Muslim countries have not yet taken any serious action to popularize the teaching of Arabic. They have been paying only lip-service to the issue in which they are expected at least to give Arabic the same status as has been enjoyed by English at all stages of education from the era of colonialism to the present time.

Enthusiasm for modern Arabic at the expense of classical Arabic is another phenomenon which has recently appeared in non-Arab Muslim countries. This is a direct result of the exclusive study of classical Arabic and the failure of the people taught by the grammar-translation method to use it in reading or writing present-day subjects. Those not familiar with the language think that there is a wide gap between classical and modern Arabic, with the former used for religious purposes, and the latter for material purposes. This is a misconception spread by the enemies of Islam for reasons revealed in a conference convened by the American Ford Foundation in Lebanon in 1973. The conference organizers and the guests chosen by the organizers insisted that academic and modern education courses require Arabic religious words to be excluded from word lists used in teaching Arabic in schools. This is nothing but an intrigue carried out against the Arab world. It was so serious that the Rector of Al-Azhar, Shaykh Abdul-Haleem Mahmoud, felt sufficiently disturbed to speak out and warn Muslims against it. It is hardly surprising to find that the intrigue is supported by those who have had Western education and are in full control of education in non-Arab Muslim countries.

(10) It should be declared explicitly and emphatically that modern Arabic type used in modern literature, newspapers, and official communications is only a branch which evolved from the classical Arabic associated with the Holy Qurān and the traditions. The branch will certainly wither and perish in any atmosphere of ignorance, corruption, and distortion created by new trends, if it does not maintain its link with classical Arabic, the Holy Qurān, and the Traditions.

Old and modern Arabic must be regarded as one body which cannot be separated. The orientalist Heyworth rightly says in his book about Modern Arabic that he has never met anybody who knows modern Arabic well without knowing classical Arabic equally well. Consequently he apologized for not writing about the history of modern Arabic literature without writing a prologue linking it with the history of old Arabic literature.

To claim that Islam and religious words are not needed for teaching Arabic is intentionally misleading, particularly when religion has a continuous influence on Muslims, in childhood and throughout life.

So far as non-Arab Muslim countries are concerned, religion is the main factor which attracts the majority of Muslims to the Arabic language. Economic and political factors, which have recently contributed to the increasing importance of Arabic at the international level, cannot, and never will, replace the religious element in the life of Muslims.

Chapter Eight

The Teaching of Languages in Muslim Universities

Muhammad Mahmood Ghaly

Born 1920 in Damietta, Egypt. Professor of English, King Abdulaziz University, Jedda. Graduated in English from Cairo University in 1940. Received a Diploma in English from Exeter University, England in 1954. Awarded M.A. (1959) and Ph.D. (1960), both in Linguistics, by the University of Michigan. Taught English in Government schools (1940–52); Lecturer in a Teachers' College (1955–61); Assistant Professor, Riyadh University (1961–64); Associate Professor and Acting Dean of Foreign Languages, Al Azhar (1965–72); joined King Abdulaziz University as Professor and Head of Department of English in 1972, was Head of Department until 1979. His publications include: *English Phonetics* (with Dr. Albert Abdullah), Cairo, 1961; *History of English* (with Dr. Albert Abdullah), Cairo, 1964; *Leaders of Linguistic Thought* (in Arabic), Jedda, 1977.

The Teaching of Languages

As a system of sounds for human communication, language is the most characteristic human activity. It gives expression to all aspects of human ideas, actions and feelings. In learning his first language, a child spends the first three years of his life mastering this marvellous tool in dealing with his environment, mainly at home. Before going to school, a normal child is fully equipped with a mastery of his native language (in one of its dialects), through which all other information at school has to be communicated.

When a child or an adult comes to learn a second language, such a favourable environment in terms of a normal family atmosphere or a concentrated effort over a number of years can never be assured. Herein lies, it would appear, two major problems in teaching a second language, namely the problem of the teacher as *model* and the problem of the need for concentrated effort. In the first category are such problems as those connected with language teaching, teacher training, and textbooks. The other category sums up all the other difficulties that face second language teaching — those of the learner, age groups and the different *social and cultural forces* at work in societies where the second language is taught.

It is beyond the scope of this paper to go into a detailed discussion of these two categories of problems since our main concern lies in the practical side of teaching second languages in Muslim universities. It seems pertinent here, however, to emphasize two important facts. Firstly, learning foreign languages is no longer a purely national matter to be decided upon by narrow national considerations, in view of the very complex matrix of international relations. Under the impact of mass media, there is a gradual shrinking of national barriers coupled with a growing intensity of ideological conflicts. In a world dominated by sheer numbers and warring ideologies, there is no place today or in the foreseeable future for *linguistic isolationism*.

There is also this important and not irrelevant fact that so much that we learn from the teaching and learning of a second language could be of immense benefit to those of us charged with the onerous and honourable task of teaching and learning *Arabic as a second language*.

Our Linguistic Commitment

The official languages at the United Nations total five: English, French, Spanish, Russian, and Chinese. Arabic has achieved only partial recognition in the United Nations, being adopted only in some specialized agencies of this world body. The approximate figures for the number of native speakers of the more important languages of the world are:

Chinese with about 800 million native speakers
English ,, ,, 350 ,, ,, ,,
Spanish ,, ,, 250 ,, ,, ,,
Arabic ,, ,, 120 ,, ,, ,,

As a second language, English has achieved global importance, with over 800 million non-native speakers. Next to English comes Arabic with at least 600 million non-native Muslims who understand the language. The implications of this important fact have never been quite clearly realized so far by most linguists and language teachers in the Muslim world.

English is spoken by about 350 million people as a first language, and by even more than double that number as a second language. Thus English offers an excellent example of linguistic commitment nationally and internationally. The scientific studies on the structure and history of English are unparalled in any other field of study concerned with an individual living language. The concentrated, unremitting and co-ordinated efforts, together with the huge budgets earmarked (in Britain and the U.S.A.) for the teaching of English as a second language present a magnificent human achievement.

But since human relations can never be only a one-direction channel, and since learning other languages is decidedly among the most fruitful means of propagating both languages and culture, keen and serious interest in learning other languages was awakened years ago in the United States. This interest was translated into large-scale programmes under the Eisenhower Act of 1957. This Act tried to fulfill the political and cultural needs of U.S. policies in the fields of foreign language teaching, with special emphasis on what it designated as critical language areas, of which Arabic was one. Needless to say, this interest in foreign languages did not stem from purely altruistic considerations. After all, the very term 'foreign' has been superseded by the term 'second' in most literature about learning other languages, to soothe the ruffled sentiments of those enormous numbers of non-native speakers of English. But the fact remains that English cannot be effectively propagated in the world without reciprocal understanding and the effective teaching of a great number of the other languages of the world. It is common knowledge now that many highly-placed officials and agents, besides native teachers of English, cannot work or teach abroad before passing tough examinations in the languages and even dialects of the areas to which they are assigned.

Similarly, our task in having to prepare teachers of Arabic who go to Muslim and non-Muslim countries alike seems to be more critical as well as more urgently needed. This means that in our universities, both Arab and non-Arab, we cannot evade the issue of learning other languages, if we are keen enough to go beyond paying hypocritical lip-service to the propagation of the language of the Holy Qurān. To assure social and cultural cohesion between different regions of the Muslim world, a native teacher of Arabic should be equipped not only with a professionally sound training in Arabic language and literature, but with a real understanding of the societies and a reasonable command of the different languages of the world which belong to Islam. This has to be complemented with co-ordinated and effective programmes for teaching Arabic in non-Arabic Muslim countries, so that Arabic can become a second language and not a very poor third or fourth.

New Orientation

The task of learning and teaching Arabic as well as other languages of the Muslim world would open before us new horizons of thought and endeavour. For centuries, the word 'progress' has cast a spell over admirers both in the West and in Muslim lands. But a definition of the word seems to be in order here. Literally, the word means 'going forward,' and if we mean by human progress this literal denotation, this is again literally true since the unfolding of human history is a progress towards an inevitable end. Progress in this sense also involves change in time and place; for as we move along, we move in both these dimensions. Old people die and new infants are born, and in this progressive change lies the secret of human existence on this earth. But when we say that 'we need reconciliation between orthodoxy and progress' (as stated in the Preamble of the First International Conference on Islamic Education), the word 'progress' defies definition in its literal meaning as well as in the Quranic sense. If by 'orthodoxy' we mean 'correct opinion', as when we say 'the Orthodox Caliphs', then orthodoxy should not be considered as the negation of progress. This is pointed out as an example of the lack of precise definitions in a domain which probably more than any other brings to the fore the dilemma of Muslim culture today. What we stand most in need of is *a reconciliation between theory and practice, between ethics and business and between word and deed*. This should be the main field of our educational *jihād*.

As Muslims, we never question the fundamentals of belief in Islam: the Oneness of Allah, the unity of prophethood, and the brotherhood of humanity. But these could never be inculcated into the Muslim mind and heart except through the basically Muslim practices of the five daily congregational prayers, and daily readings of the glorious Qurān. Here is the way for our progress, our salvation and our glory. Any other way inevitably leads to frustration and destruction.

The apparent apathy towards such regular performances in the past on the part of the élite in most Muslim countries can be very effectively remedied if we keep in mind the ominous fact that the orthodox Companions and the Blessed Prophet himself considered such negligence a sure sign of hypocrisy. In Islam, hypocrisy is sometimes worse than outright disbelief.

The regular performance of these heavenly injunctions is the hope not only for progress, salvation, and glory of Muslims, but for the progress, salvation and glory of the whole of humanity.

The Place of English in Muslim Education

English is a world language. This is a fact of the modern world, mainly because it represents the power and influence of the English-speaking people in the fields of science, politics, economics and cultural and military achievements. To stop teaching English is to sever the ties between ourselves and the modern civilized world. But we should also desist from indulging in the self-deceptive notion that our boys and girls should expect to work, feel, and think with English hands, hearts and minds.

Ever since 1936 (1355) the proposal for conducting all instruction in the higher education of the Arab world in the language of the Holy Qurān has been on the agenda of policy makers awaiting implementation. It is high time that it should be implemented. Any excuses for dodging the issue are again signs of our deep-rooted hypocritical yearning for the line of least resistance. After all, bilingualism should never be achieved at the expense of our cultural survival.

The Al-Azhar Experiment

Our age-old honoured institution of worship and learning, the Al-Azhar, has been subjected to an 'evolutionary' or 'progressive' experiment. With the growing religious consciousness in Egypt and the Muslim world, the idea of modernizing Al-Azhar had been gaining momentum. In 1961 the New Order or Law for Al-Azhar was adopted, and now after so many years the experiment is worthy of study.

It is beyond our scope here to deal with the New Law concerning the introduction of new subjects besides the traditionally-taught subjects in the Primary, Preparatory and Secondary schools of Al-Azhar. But in passing, it should be noted that the newly introduced subjects have resulted in an extremely crowded syllabus, too exacting for both students and teachers; an even balance between both types of learning not having yet been reached.

The story has been different with the traditional College of Al-Azhar University. The approach here was different, because new Colleges for Medicine, Engineering, Science, Agriculture, Education and Languages were established and were added to the three older Colleges of Muslim Law, Theology and Arabic. These new institutions were steps in the right direction, but they were only one third of the battle for rejuvenation, or what is wrongly termed 'modernization'; for rejuvenation should also involve bringing new life to the systems of instruction in the three older colleges, a step which could never have been regarded as easy. To change the system of instruction in these three colleges is tantamount to a change in the orientation of our culture, which cannot be achieved except as a large-scale programme to be worked out gradually with persistence and vision.

A third dimension of the change has been the new emphasis on learning other languages. As a modest beginning, a small Institute of Languages and Translation was set up, which has become a full-fledged College, with seven departments of European, Eastern and African languages.

A corollary of this whole programme would be to introduce serious courses on Arabic and Islam in all the other universities and colleges of Egypt with the hope that an eventual unity of approach and outlook in all institutions of learning could be achieved. This whole programme has not yet been completed, but it can serve as a model for a new orientation where similar attempts are envisaged in other Arab and Muslim countries.

A rough outline of a co-ordinated programme for the teaching of languages under such a project would run as follows:

I Intermediate (Preparatory) Schools

Arabic and no other language should be taught up to the end of the Intermediate or Preparatory stages. The time now allotted to other languages should be given to the study of these major cultural and linguistic areas:

A. Arabic and Muslim culture.
B. History and culture of other peoples in Asia, Africa, Europe and the Americas.

II Secondary Schools

Other language teaching should be started from the first year of secondary school, and the other languages to be taught could be divided into these groups:
A. European languages: English, French, Spanish and German.

B. Islamic languages: Turkish, Persian, Urdu, Bengali, Indonesian, Malaysian.
C. African and Eastern languages: Bantu, Swahili, Hausa and other languages of interest.

A student would have to choose two languages besides Arabic and his own language. The first two years of study in secondary schools should carry nine hours weekly (six and three hours respectively) for these two languages. In the third year the number of hours should be raised to twelve — eight and four respectively. In the latter case it would serve the purpose best if a new branch for languages could be established in the General Certificate of Secondary Education in addition to the two already existing branches of Literary and Scientific.

III Higher Education

A. A greater variety of languages should be offered at this stage; it would be contrary to the spirit of our age, contrary to our cultural commitments, and even contrary to our linguistic commitment to the language of the Holy Qurān, to have one language department, that of English, in almost all our institutions of higher education.

At least three departments of languages should be opened in all full-fledged universities:
1. A Department of European Languages.
2. A Department of Islamic Languages.
3. A Department of African and Eastern Languages.

B. As language is the medium, key, and mirror of culture, the teaching of other languages should not be separated from the general culture and historical matrix of the country as a whole.

C. A greater emphasis should be placed upon learning the basic structure of the languages studied rather than on the study of literature before the essentials of the language are under complete control. Here the use of modern audio-visual aids should form an integral part of the courses.

D. A second language should always be a *second* language. Our students should never be tempted into the delusion of trying to have a foreign language for their own first and native language.

We can no longer afford that waste of time, effort, and energy on a luxurious mirage of subservience to an alien culture. Our first languague should be given highest priority in all programmes for higher education, if we are really keen to have *good translators* who can efficiently and honestly do the job of rendering our Arabic heritage into the other languages of the Muslim and non-Muslim world, and who can also turn into Arabic the best that has been produced in other languages. One example here is in order, the Glorious Qurān itself. We have been learning and teaching English for the last hundred years, and no acceptable rendering of the meanings of the Glorious Qurān into English is still within sight. It might be argued that we might have been awed by the stupenduous task of rendering such a Divine revelation. But besides this Book nearly all the works on science and technology in foreign languages and all the vast heritage of our past are still awaiting good translators. We should not have to entrust foreign orientalists and missionaries with the job. *It will not do to try to be native speakers of English. We have to know Arabic better, and other languages better, too.*
E. These university programmes could be supplemented in time with higher courses leading to M.A. and Ph.D. degrees in Language, Literature and Translation, and these would include field trips to the countries where the languages are spoken as mother tongues.

Finally, these suggestions in very broad outline may serve as guidelines for a more detailed discussion of a concrete plan of action. But an agreement in principle is indispensable. For we have learnt from the lessons of our early, as well as our recent, history that in political and economic systems as well as in education, the differing forms of the system do not matter so long as the content is truly Islamic. The tragic events of recent decades have left engraved in our memories the fact that the means do not justify the end because means and end have to share in the sublime purity and the noble honesty of the sacred cause of Divine Relevation.

Now with the growth of Muslim wealth, which eventually means power, it is the duty of all of us to explore with determination and vision the ways and means of dedicating this power to the service of Islam.

If, coupled with this realization of our newly acquired material power, our educated community who are Muslims in name only are changed into an educated community of practising Muslims, then we shall be able to respond to the Divine Call of the noble Messenger, and then the world will inevitably listen to the magnificent message of the Glorious Qurān.

Appendix

Recommendations of the Committee on Philosophy, Literature, and the Arts

Considering the importance of philosophy, literature and the arts in any Islamic educational system, and the changes which the Islamic world faces from the loss of the Islamic character of these disciplines the following recommendations are proposed:

I. Philosophy

a) Muslim students should first be provided with a firm foundation in Islamic philosophy and thought in general and only then exposed to modern Western philosophy. Moreover, all other philosophical schools should be taught and studied from the point of view of Islamic philosophy.
b) Students should not be exposed to modern science before having acquaintance with the Islamic philosophy and conception of sciences and the history of Islamic science.
c) Attention should be paid to the rational criticism of Western science by Western thinkers themselves, such as the scientific and rational refutation of evolution and other similar suppositions by Western scientists themselves, and also to the criticism of one modern philosophical school by another. The study of the sciences should in any case be always accompanied by an inquiry into their suppositions and methods.
d) Special emphasis should be laid at the High School level on the intellectual understanding of the Islamic revelation.

II. Literature

a) Programmes for the translation of the masterpieces of Islamic literature from one Islamic language to another should be devised.
b) Centres should be established for the translation of writings from other civilisations into various Islamic languages, as well as of the intellectual treasures of Islam into non-Islamic languages.
c) A systematic study should be made of the influence of Islamic thought upon Western thought and literature.
d) Special programmes should be devised to translate the masterpieces of Islamic languages into other languages, but in a highly literary form and as literature.
e) The teaching of the main Islamic languages and literatures should be encouraged in all Islamic universities
f) A genuinely Islamic school of literary criticism and Islamic aesthetics based on Islamic principles should be developed, which could provide criteria for the study of various forms of literature with which Muslims are becoming acquainted.
g) The organization and execution should be undertaken of an extensive programme for the preservation and cataloguing of Islamic manuscripts, providing services for making them available to scholars and providing means to edit and publish as many of these manuscripts as possible, starting with those which are most important in their own field.

III. Arts and Crafts

Recognising that the arts and crafts which have been developed by Muslims since the very beginning of their history fulfil an essential role for the *ummah*, inasmuch as they shape the frame of material life so that it reflects the beauty of the revealed Message and inasmuch as they form an integral component of the Islamic way of life;

considering that the invasion by industrial products together with social, economic and cultural disruptions have brought about a serious decadence of traditional arts and crafts throughout the Islamic World;

conscious of the fact that the degradation and final elimination of these arts and crafts would entail an immense loss for the Muslim

World, which would be left to live in an environment deprived of its genuine Islamic quality;

conscious also that the disappearance of the traditional artists and craftsmen who have always played an important role in the maintenence and propagation of the Islamic faith would be of disastrous consequence for the equilibrium of the *ummah*;

it is resolved that the following steps be taken:

Education of the general public in Islamic arts and crafts

a) A sense of the value and beauty of traditional art forms should be imparted as far as possible to all members of the Islamic community, so as to counter the contemporary trend which tends to consider art as the prerogative of an élite and to separate it from ordinary life.
b) The disruptive influence exerted by aggressive forms of music recently imported from the West should be resisted.
c) Mass-media should allot more room in their programmes for the presentation of the riches of Islamic art.
d) Other means of education of the public should include lectures and discussions, temporary and permanent exhibitions and demonstrations, and regular cultural tours organized for national and foreign visitors to handicraft quarters.
e) The traditional apprenticeship system which has proved its efficiency throughout the centuries should be maintained wherever possible. However, due to many recent adverse factors, this system should receive some assistance on the part of public authorities, notably in the form of stipends and facilities for the complementary general education of the craftsmen.
f) The creation of 'government apprenticeship centres' where children are admitted after completion of their primary school should also be encouraged provided that control is exercised of the level of skill reached by the pupils during their training.
g) The creation of special schools of traditional arts and crafts should be encouraged in all Islamic countries. The aim of such institutions would be to form an élite of craftsmen possessing a good level of general and technical education, as well as a high standard of skill in the various branches of traditional art. Such craftsmen would be called on, *inter alia*, to participate in rehabilitation programmes undertaken in Islamic cities and on Islamic monuments.

Higher education in the arts and crafts and the cultural heritage of Islam

    h) At the higher or university level, a great effort is needed to develop new patterns of education in the departments of art, the faculties of architecture and in general, all the branches of the 'humanities' where students need to be familiarized with the aesthetic principles that underline Islamic art.

Programmes of national and inter-Islamic character

    i) The development of an inter-Islamic fund and organization to carry out the necessary steps for the preservation and rehabilitation of the Islamic cities from the point of view both of their architecture and city planning and of the life in them, such as intellectual life, and traditional arts and crafts.

    j) To include in all programmes for the revival of the Islamic educational system elements devoted to education in arts and the crafts, and to the familiarization of all students at all levels with their traditional artistic heritage.

    k) To encourage and help in every possible way those international organisations such as UNESCO which are carrying out programmes in the study and preservation of Islamic cities and Islamic arts and crafts, and help to co-ordinate such programmes.

    l) To hold an inter-Islamic conference as soon as possible to coordinate efforts and to propose a programme of action; and to study the means of establishing the permanent organization mentioned in the Resolution.

    m) The encouragement of authorities in all Islamic countries to construct educational and public buildings according to the principles and in the tradition of Islamic architecture.

    n) The meaning of Islamic art should be expounded in such a way as to emphasize its spritual character and its intimate link with the principles of the Islamic Revelation; and those forms of art should be encouraged which are in conformity with the spirit and the norms of Islamic art, such as calligraphy, traditional geometrical design, and architecture.

    o) Donations and awards should be instituted to encourage studies, research work, publications and the crafts, as well as

the various branches of Islamic culture both written and oral.
p) Every effort should be made to revive the function of the craftsman and artist and to reinstate respect for him as it existed in traditional Islamic society.
q) Oral traditions which over the years have been an important means for the transmission of Islamic culture should be preserved in every way possible.
r) Wherever possible, centres of Islamic art should be established in conjunction with the activities of living centres of arts and crafts, and with the education of the young in Islamic art.
s) In countries which have adopted other scripts such as the Latin and the Cyrillic, every attempt should be made to teach the Arabic and Persian scripts as widely as possible starting at the primary school level.

IV. Special Resolution on the Islamic City

The Islamic city has always been the heart and centre of Islamic civilization where sciences have been cultivated and arts have received their finest expression, and where the Islamic pattern of life has become totally blended with the architecture, city planning, irrigation, technology, trade, and commerce, as well as with the specifically religious and cultural aspects of life, into an organized entity and totality which is the most palpable expression of the unity lying at the heart of the Islamic Revelation. Therefore, the First International Conference on Muslim Education cannot remain indifferent to the fate of the Islamic city where in fact most of Islamic education has been carried out throughout history and which, in itself, is an embodiment of the ideas of Islamic education and the locus for the transmission of Islamic culture.

Today, the great Islamic cities, these most precious elements of the Islamic heritage, are facing the gravest danger since the rise of Islamic civilization itself, paralleling, and even surpassing, the Mongol invasion or natural disasters. This danger often arises out of action in the name of organization and modernization as well as industrial development, but almost always upon Western models which are totally alien and opposed to the Islamic conception of life as well as to the ecological equilibrium which the Islamic way of life has always emphasized. Moreover, most of these developments, in addition to the destruction of the natural environment and the dissipation of energy and natural resources of the countries involved, have caused psychological dislocation, disruption of family life and social ties upon which the Islamic way of life is based, as well as the creation of an atmosphere full of ugliness which is totally opposed to the genius of Islamic civilization and which results in an ever-increasing degree of spiritual unhappiness and moral and social degeneration. To prevent these destructive tendencies from developing any further the following for the preservation of Islamic cities is proposed:

Special Resolution on the Holy Cities of Makkah and Medina

In view of the rapid rate of urban planning and development in the Kingdom of Saudi Arabia and out of fear that such drastic changes will obliterate the centuries-old pristine and Islamic character of the two Holy cities of Mecca and Medina, and consistent with its desire to preserve their ecology and character for future generations, the First World Conference on Muslim Education proposes the following recommendations:

a) Care has to be taken to preserve the character of Makkah and Medina and to keep their natural settings as God has created them.
b) Work has to be undertaken for the preservation of the Islamic heritage in their buildings and inherited crafts.
c) Modern mechanical devices or machines that will have an adverse effect on the character of the Holy Places and the Spirit of the *Hajj* must be avoided. However, the best and most effective scientific means should be found to maintain cleanliness and sanitation in the above-mentioned cities without changing the ecological balance in them.
d) King Abdul Aziz University should be urged to form a team of Muslim experts in relevant disciplines such as religion, architecture, engineering, history and sociology to carry out research and studies on the *Hajj* and the Holy places with the purpose of finding the best ways for the development and preservation of the Islamic religious nature of those places.
e) The plans for the development of the two Holy Cities in the light of the findings of the research and the study already available should be reconsidered.